DOUBLE-PEDAL GOLD

★★★★★

A comprehensive series of exercises for developing double-pedal technique

DISCARDED BY
MEMPHIS PUBLIC LIBRARY

By Joe Morton

Written by Joe Morton

Edited by Steve Ferraro

Design by MG Design

Music Engraving by Nick Seip and Steve Ferraro

Executive Producers: Paul Siegel and Rob Wallis

ISBN: 1423425979
HL06620112
HD-BK-12

www.hudsonmusic.com
© 2007 Hudson Music

THIS BOOK IS DEDICATED TO THE ALL IN ALL

And to everyone who has helped, influenced, or inspired me in my lifetime.

My thanks and gratitude go out to so many people who helped and inspired this work.

Thanks to all the students who kept on demanding to learn the double pedal.

Thanks to Rick for the inspiration and friendship.

Thanks to Gary for sharing all the knowledge and friendship.

Thanks to Mark for his time and consultation.

Thanks to Patrick for all his help.

Thanks to all who get this book and study.

Finally, thanks to whatever it was that led me to play drums. In many aspects, it has been such a positive influence in my life. A person playing drums can turn negative emotions, such as anger, pain, fear, and resentment, into positive and even artistic release. This can increase one's confidence and self-esteem.

Joe Morton

Joe Morton

joemorton@doublepedalgold.com

INTRODUCTION

This book presents fun, exciting, and challenging exercises for the double-pedal or single-pedal drummer.*

The purpose of this book is to give the player the ability to execute rolls on the bass drum. There are no right or left designations, as I feel it is up to the player to find his or her own comfort zone as to stickings, or in this case footings.

I use double strokes on almost all 32nd-notes and many 16th-note patterns, as this is my comfort zone.

I hope the exercises, patterns, and solos in this book will spark your imagination and give rise to your own ideas and help you become a better drummer.

I hope you enjoy this book. Practice and you will accomplish your goals!

* For single-pedal drummers, all that is necessary is to change all 32nd-notes to 16th-notes.

NOTATION KEY

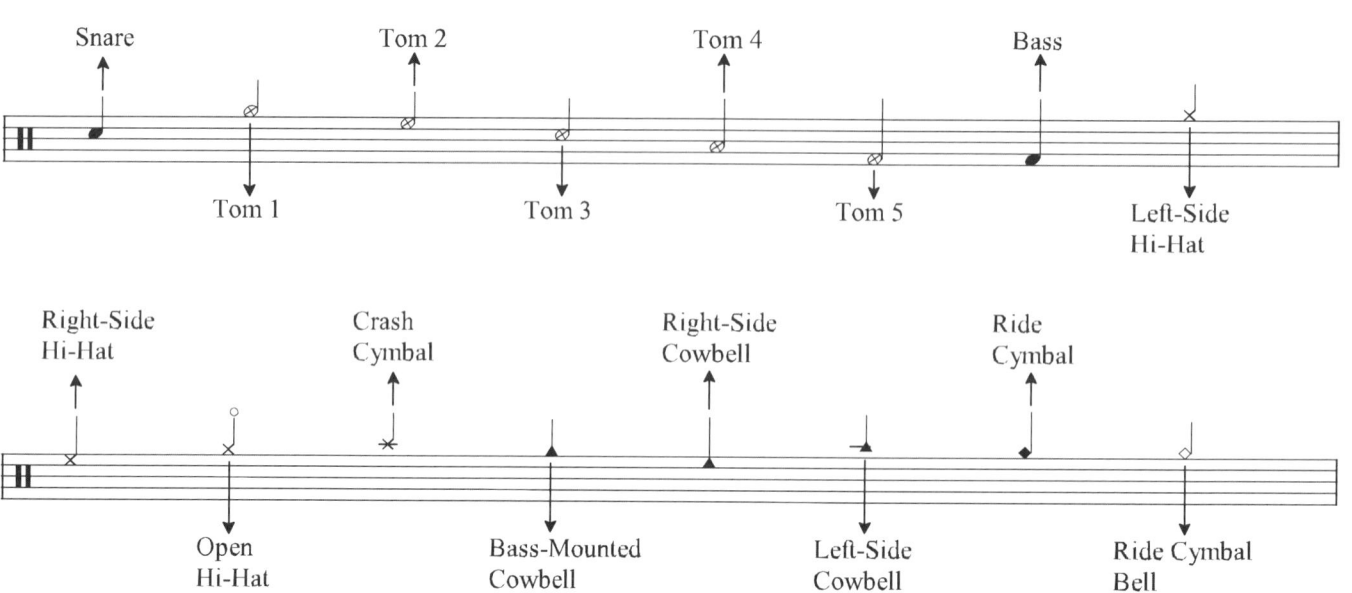

JOE MORTON

TABLE OF CONTENTS

NOTATION KEY	4
PREPARATORY EXERCISES	6
HAND-FOOT EXERCISES	6
DOUBLE STROKES	8
TRIPLETS	10
DRUMSET HAND-FOOT PATTERNS	12
GROOVE PATTERNS	17
TRIPLET GROOVE PATTERNS	20
BEATS WITH 16TH-NOTES	21
HAND OVERLAYS	22
BEATS WITH 32ND-NOTES	25
FOR MY SINGLE-PEDAL FRIENDS	34
SOLOS	36

PREPARATORY EXERCISES

These exercises will help develop endurance and coordination with the feet. Play each exercise with the right foot only, then with the left foot only, then play both feet together.

1
2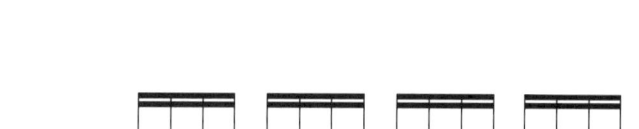

3
4

5
6

7
8

HAND-FOOT EXERCISES

These exercises are to be played with the hands and the feet.

1
2

3
4

5
6

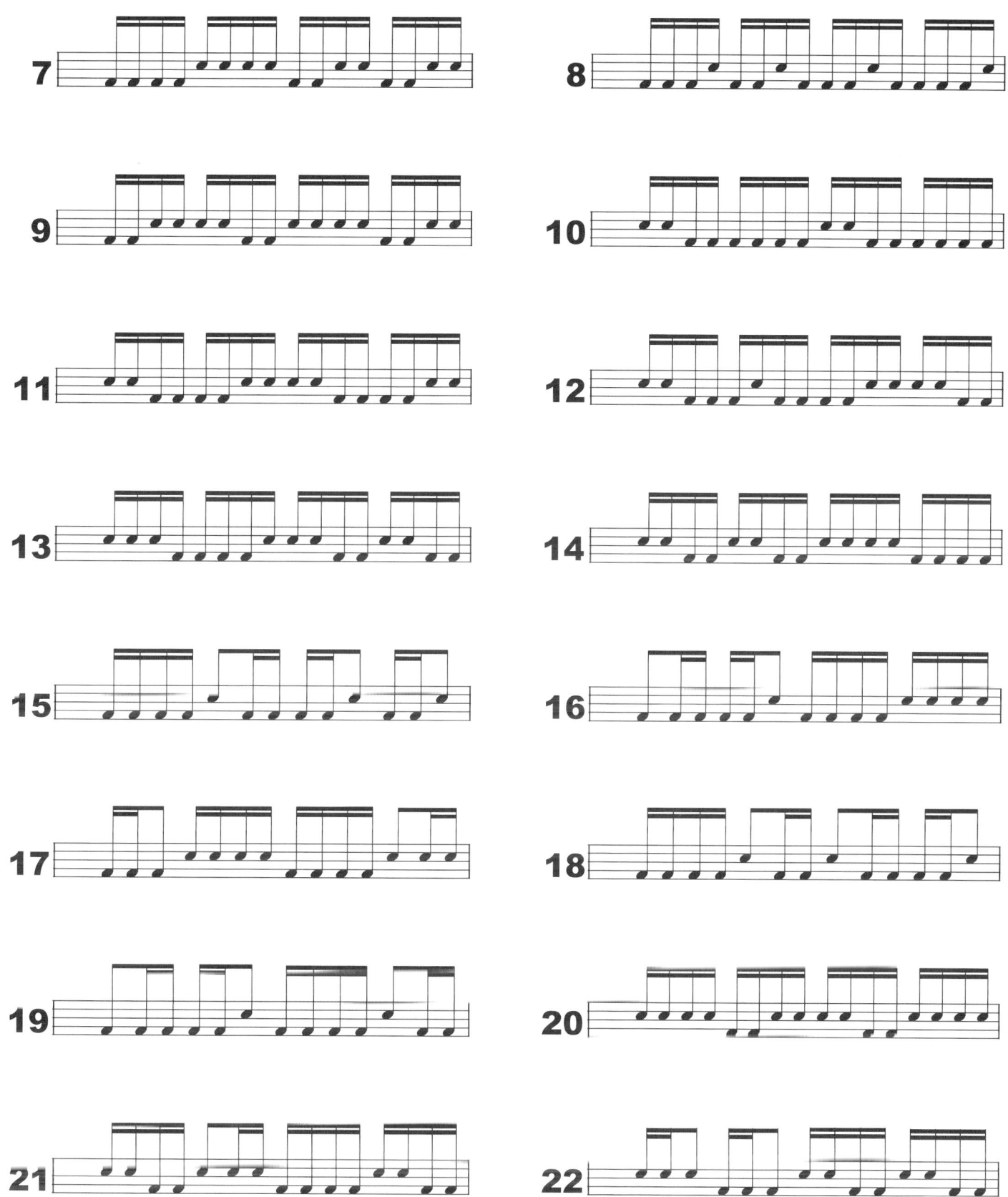

DOUBLE STROKES

These exercises prepare you (the player) to execute double-strokes with each foot. Play each pattern with the feet, then play each exercise as a groove, using 8th-notes on the hi-hat and "two" and "four" on the snare. The slashed notes within the 16th-note groupings are 32nd-notes. These notes are to be played as double-strokes on the bass pedals.

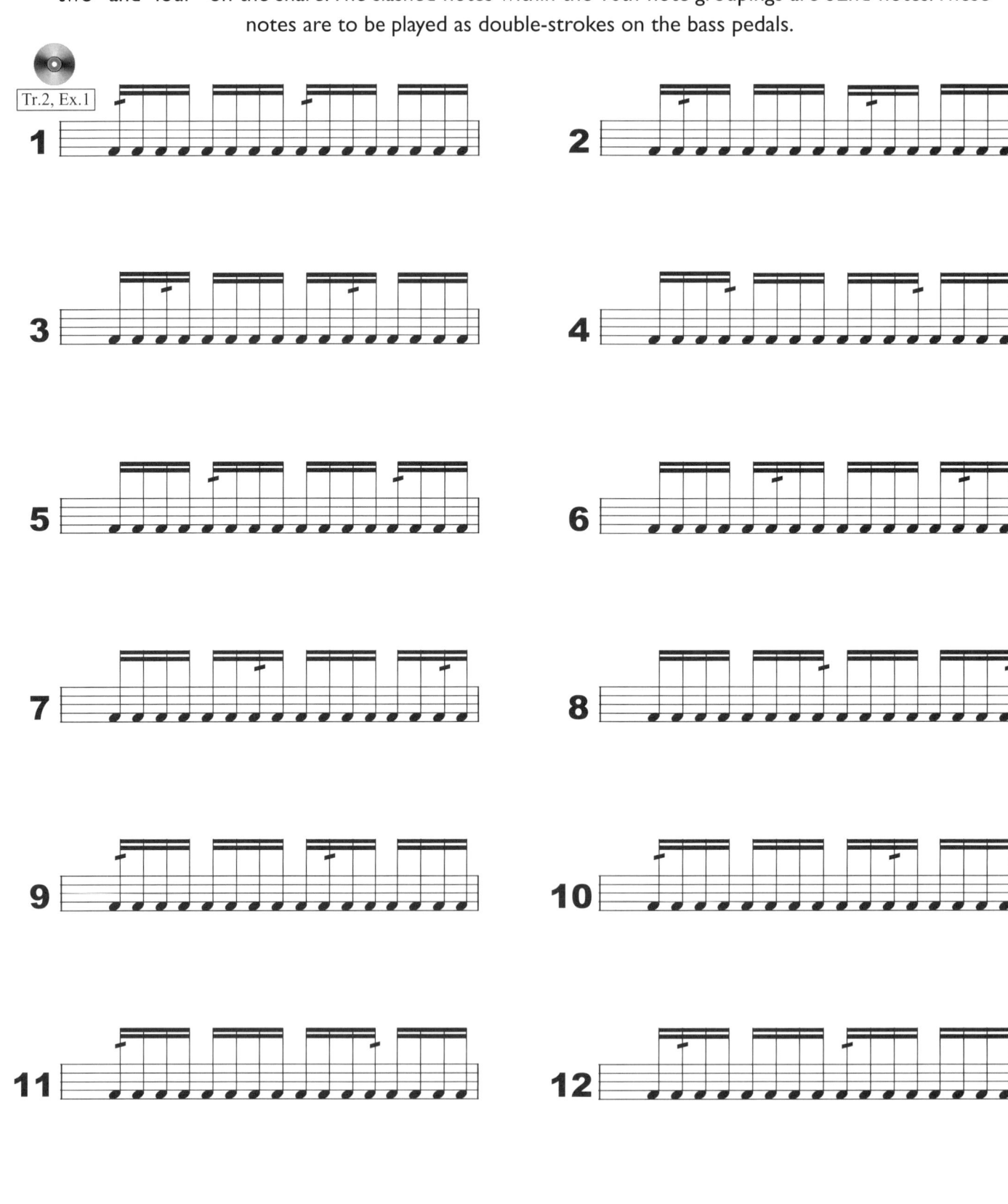

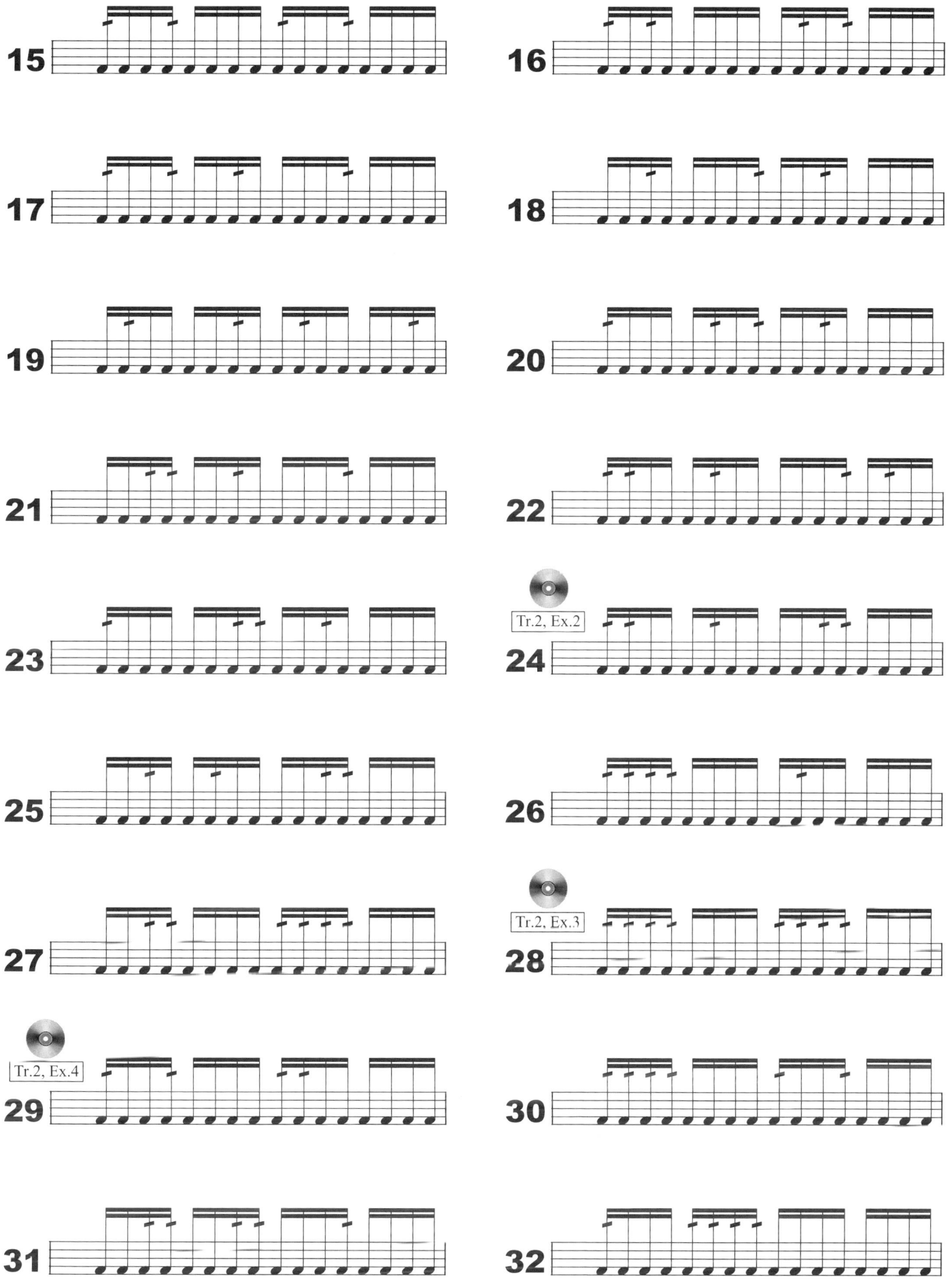

TRIPLETS

Play quarter-notes on the hi-hat when playing these exercises as a groove.

Tr.3, Ex.1

1    2

3 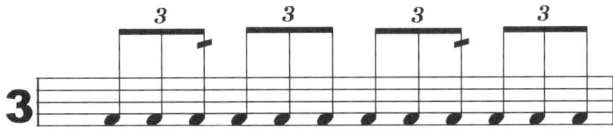   4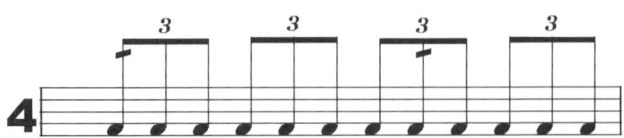

5 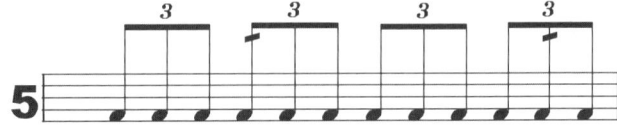   6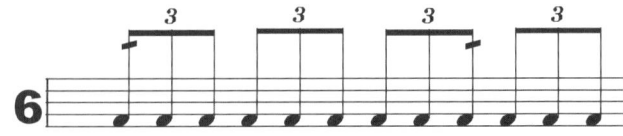

7    8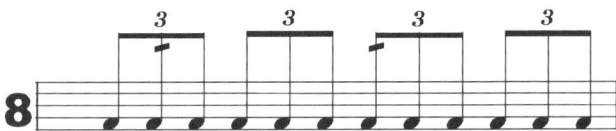

9 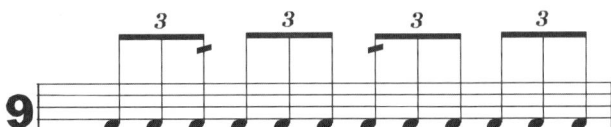   10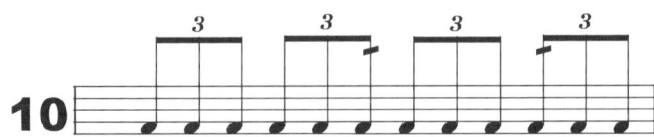

Tr.3, Ex.2

11 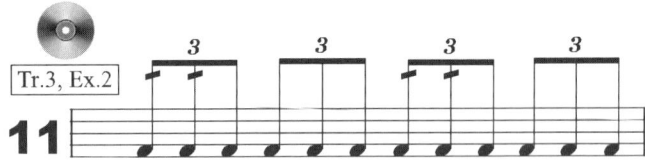   12

13 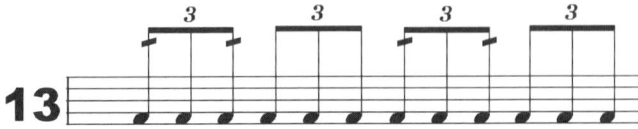   14

15    16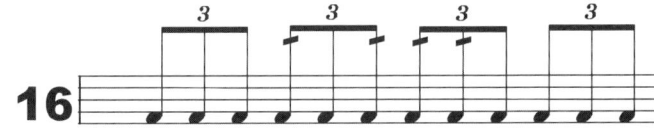

10 JOE MORTON

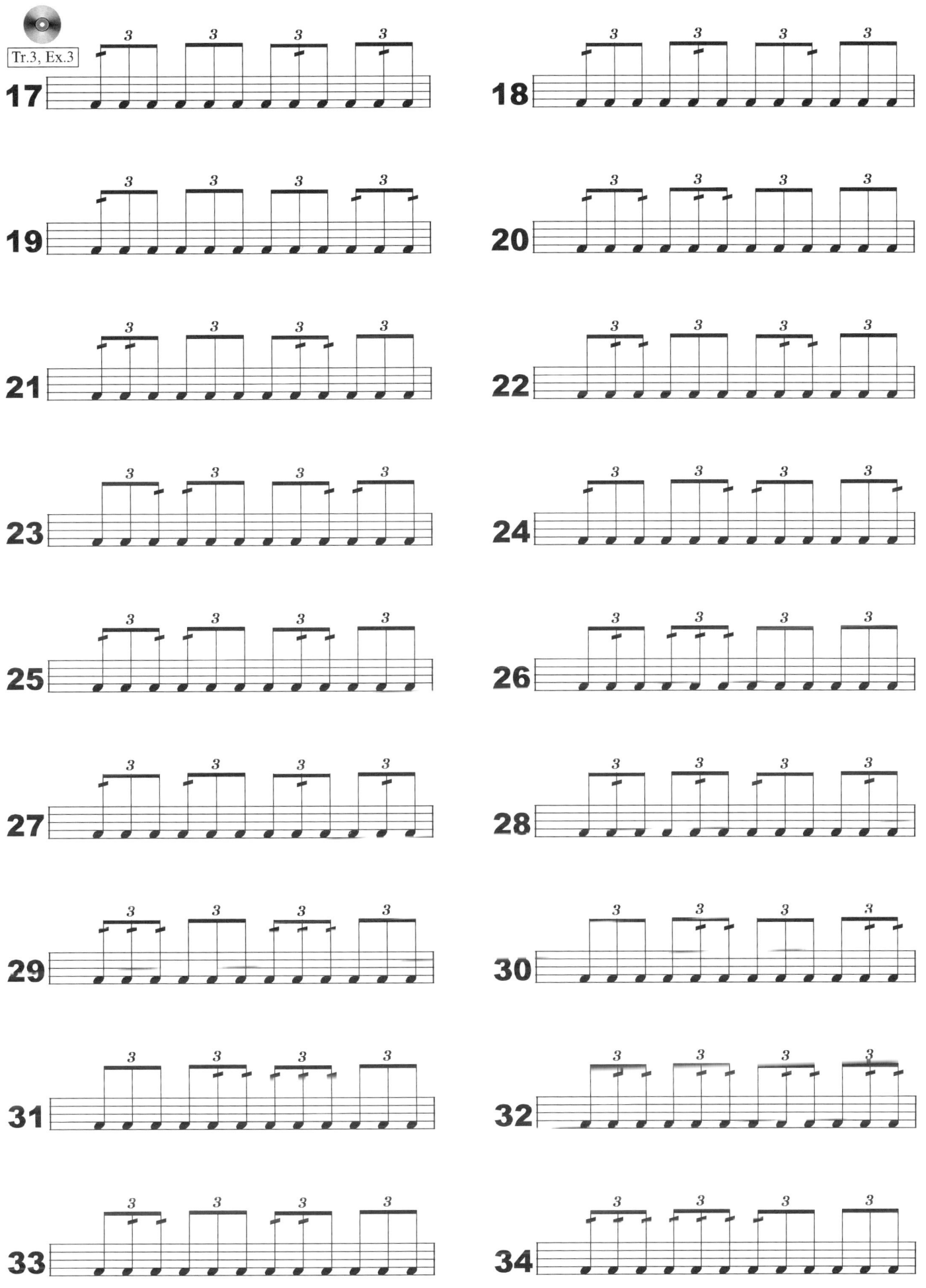

DRUMSET HAND-FOOT PATTERNS

Play the bass drum part as singles, doubles, or both.

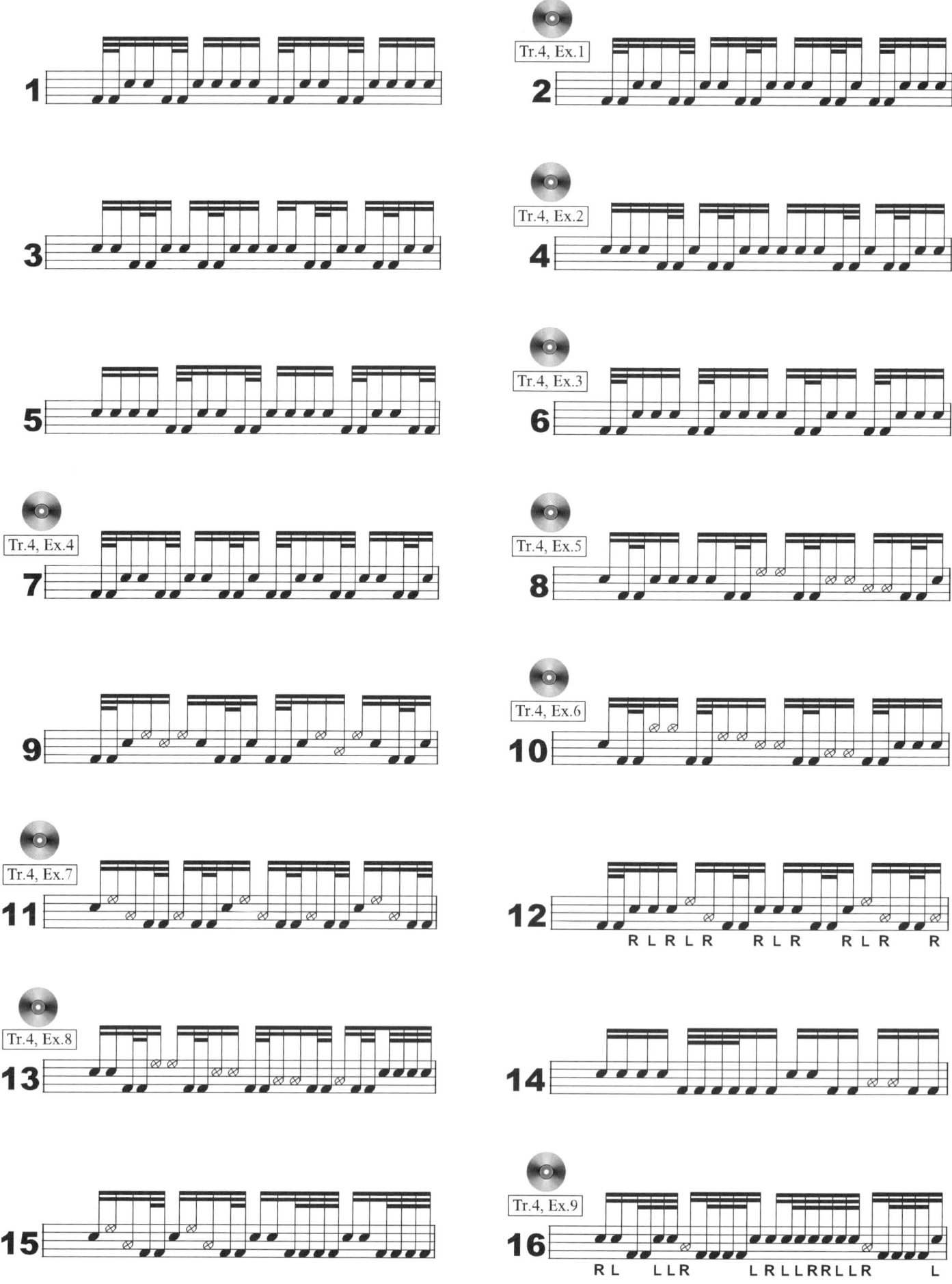

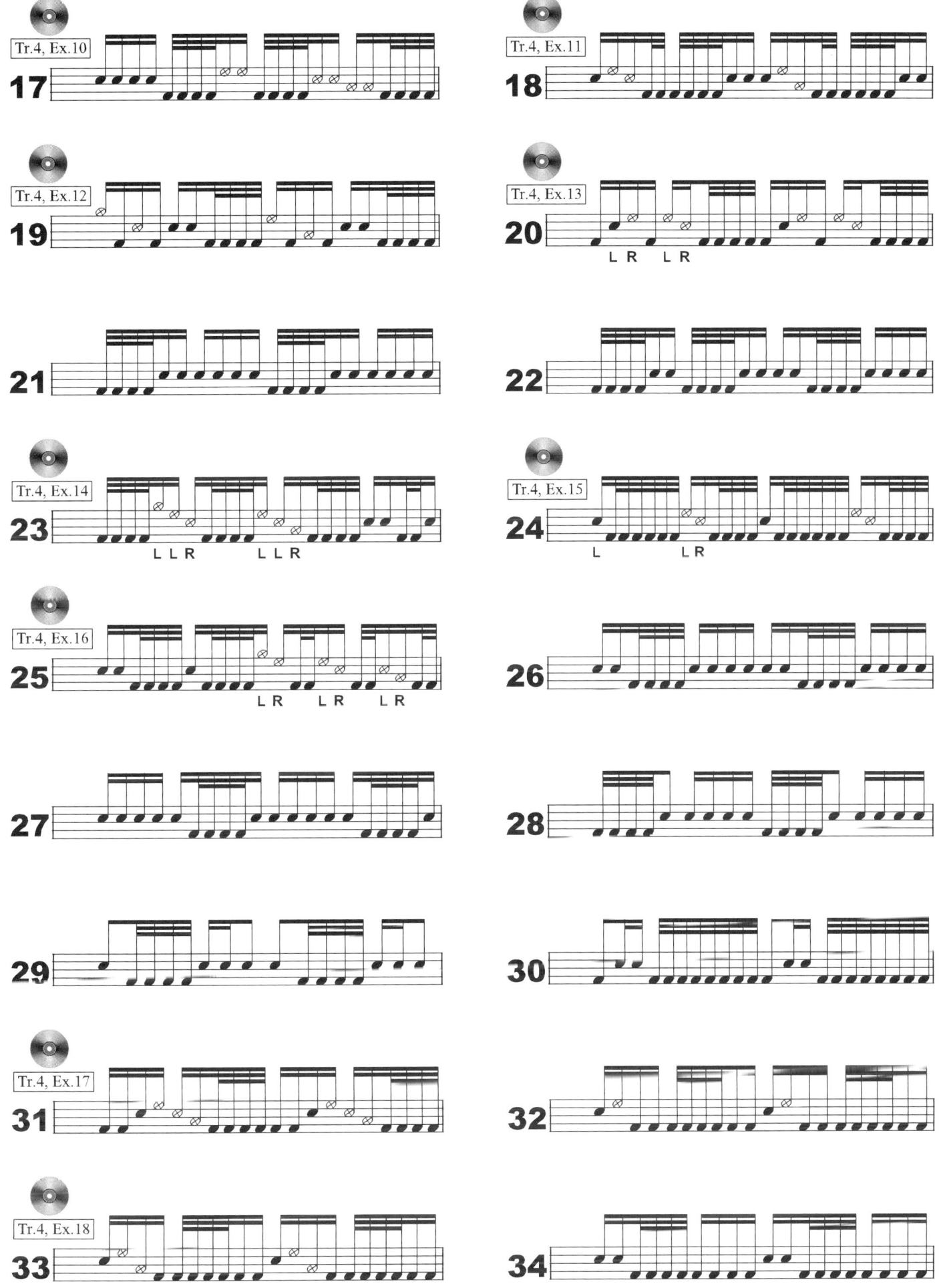

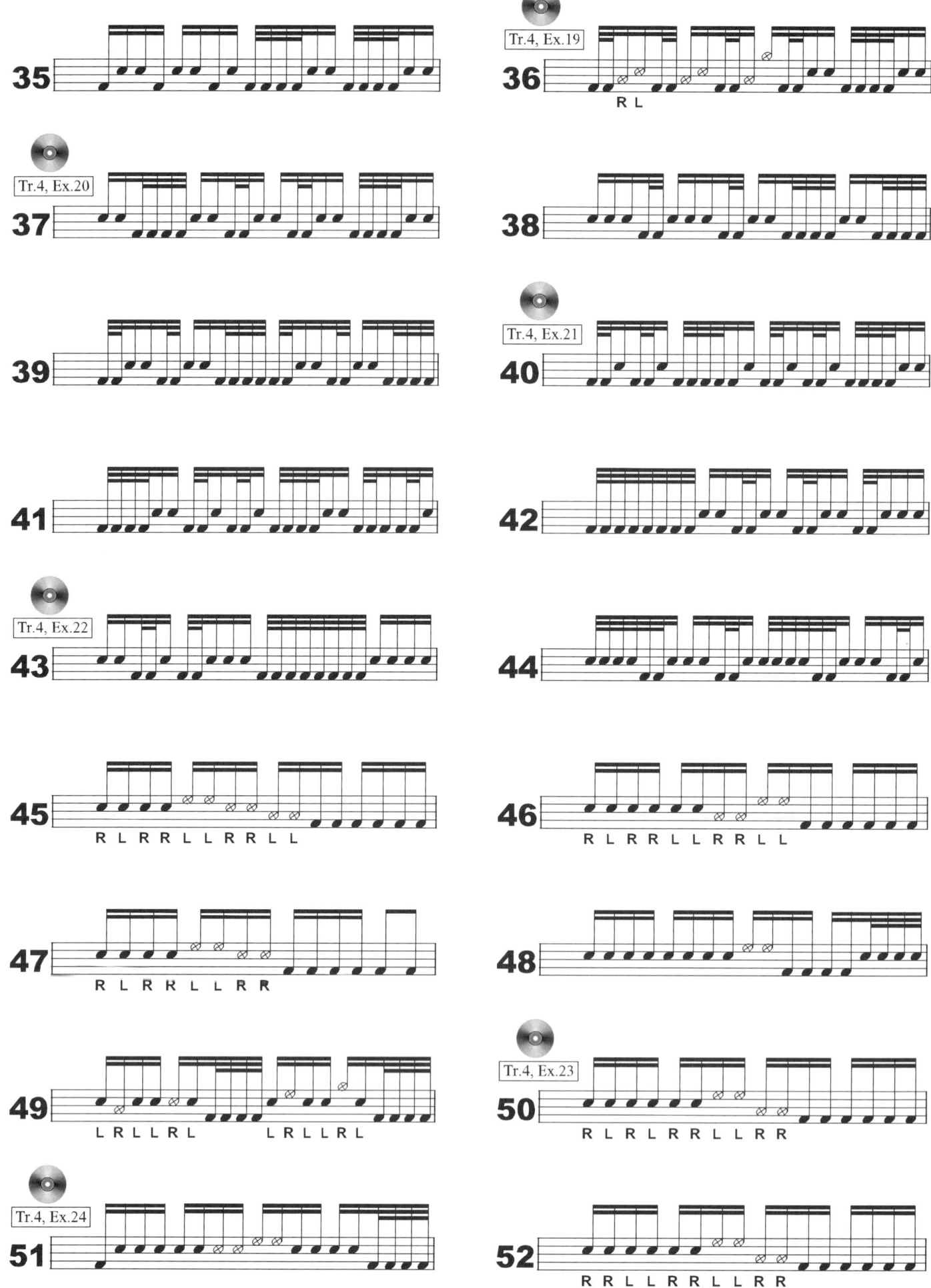

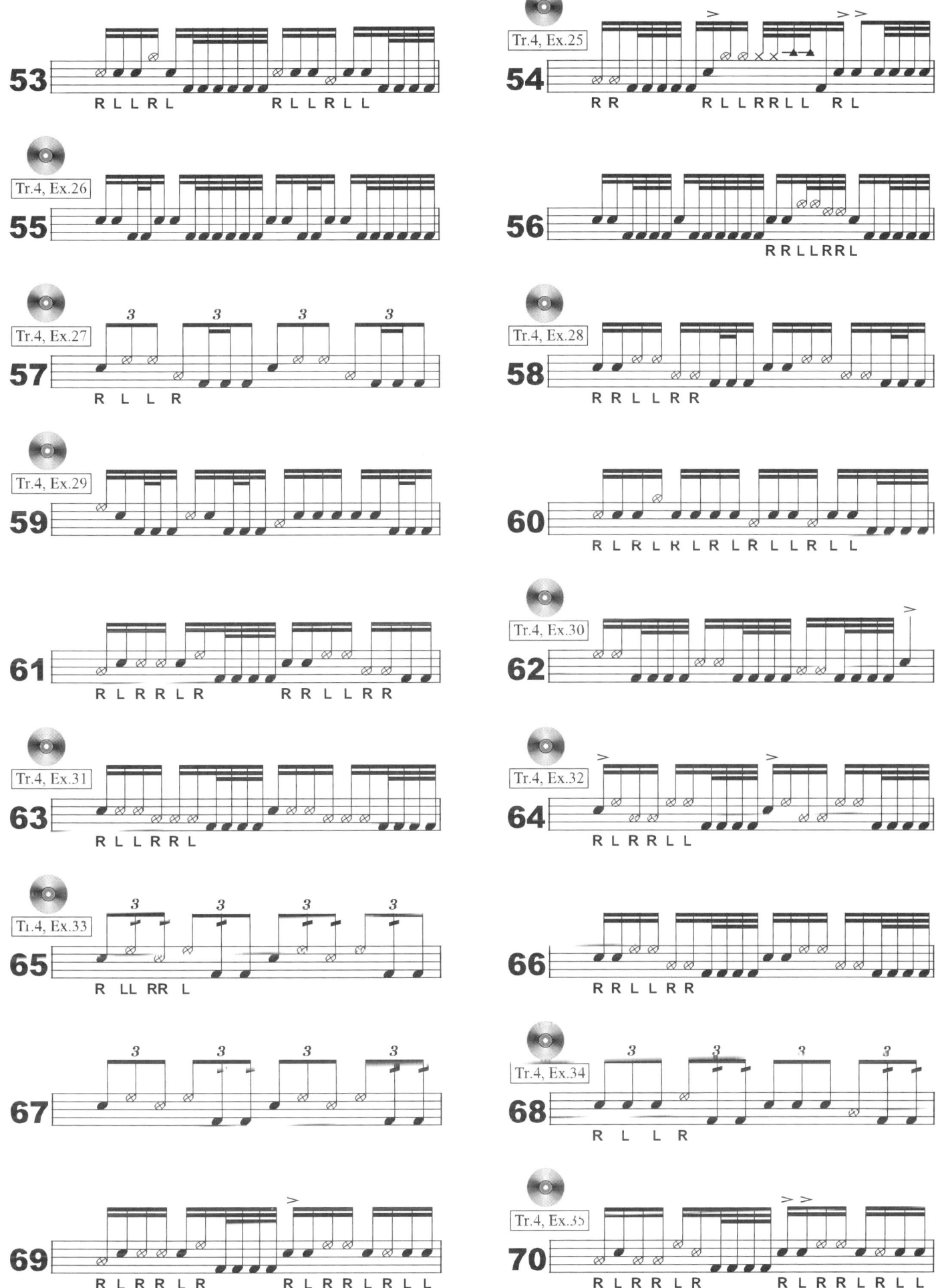

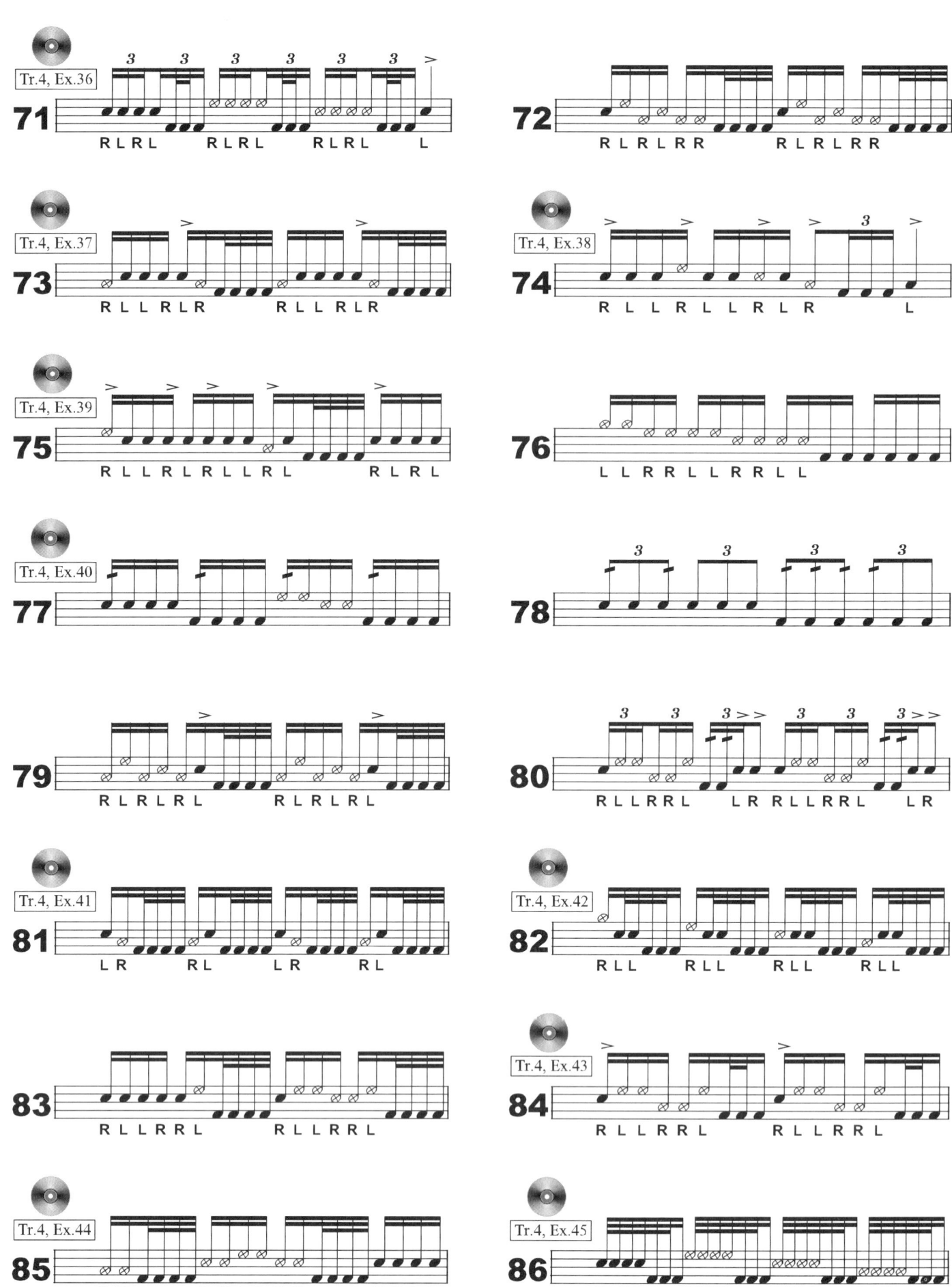

GROOVE PATTERNS

Accents are for the snare only.

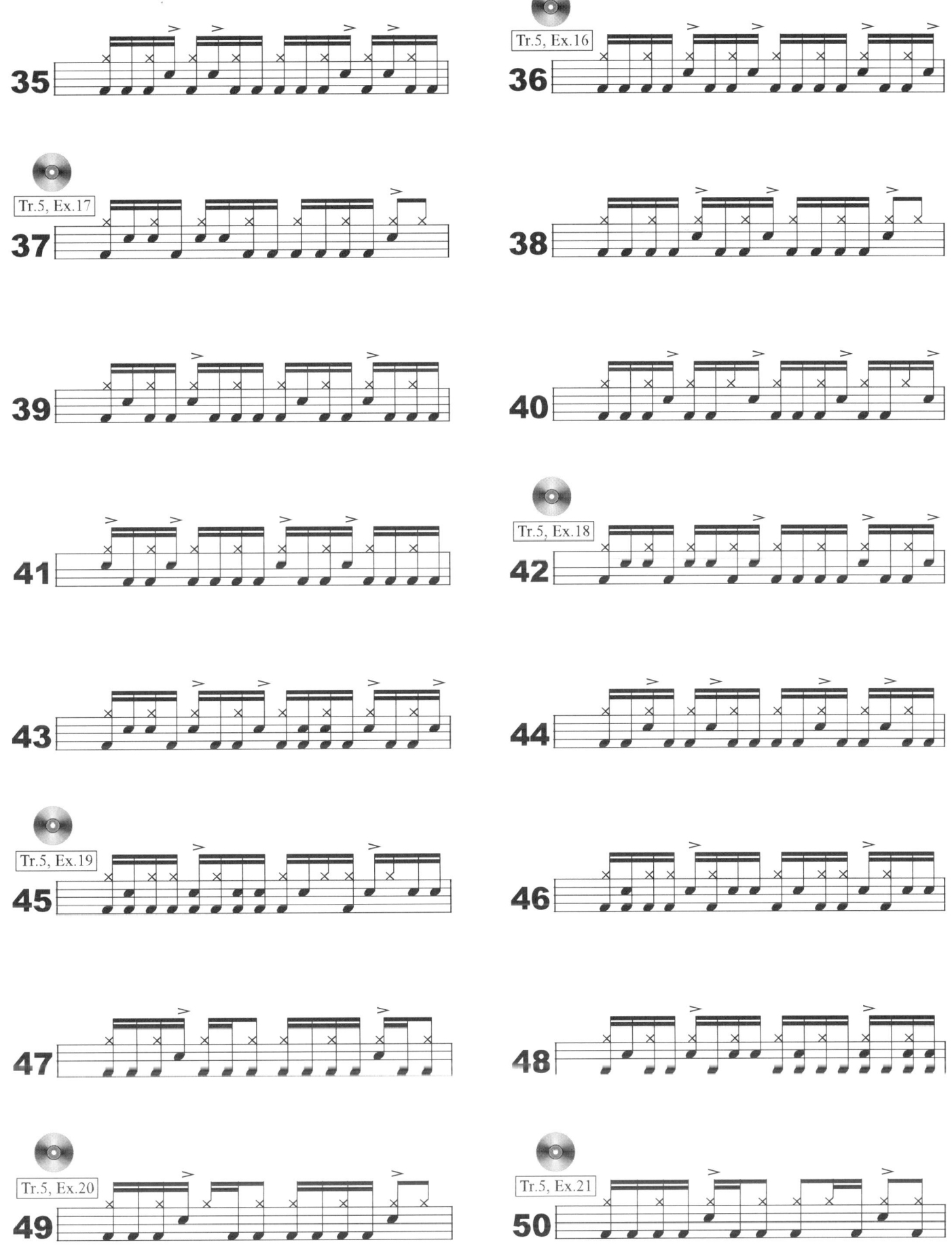

TRIPLET GROOVE PATTERNS

Accents and stickings are for the snare only.

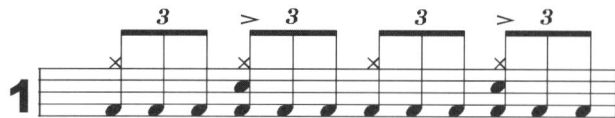
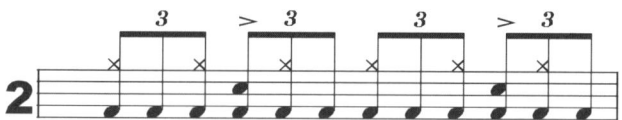
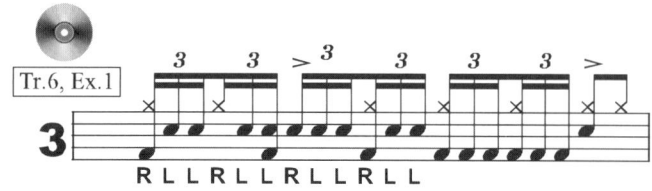
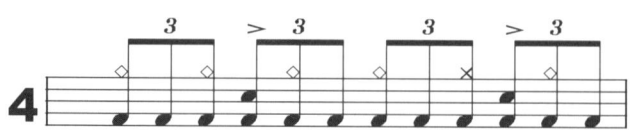
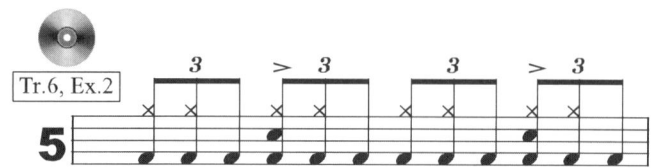
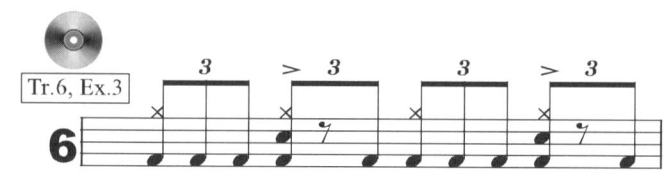

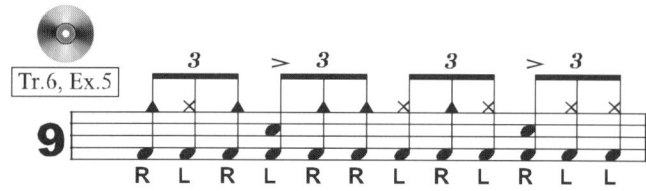
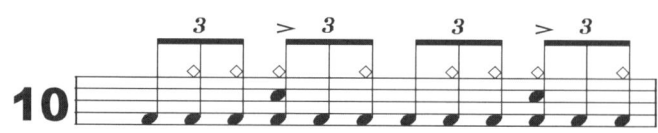
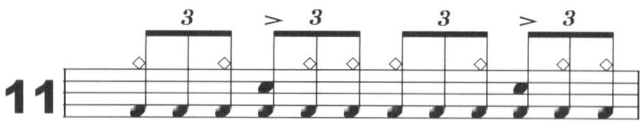
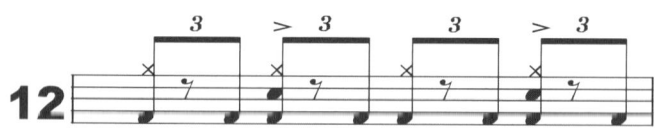
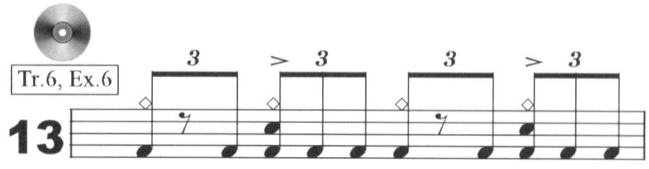

20 JOE MORTON

BEATS WITH 16TH-NOTES

Accents are for the snare and toms only.

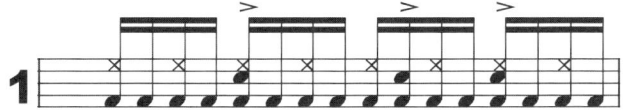

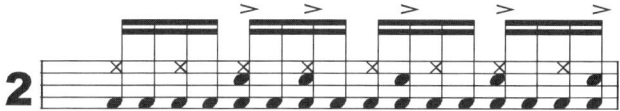

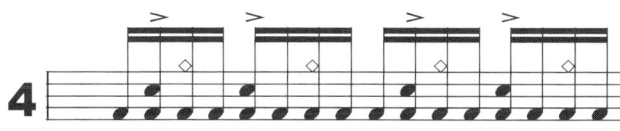

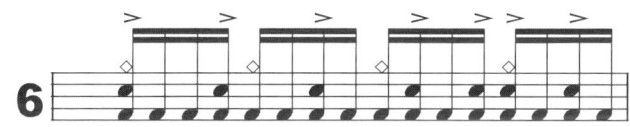

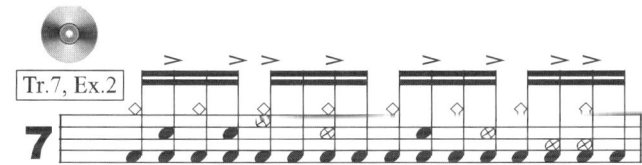

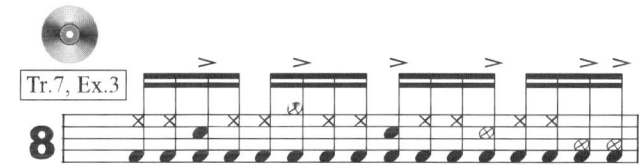

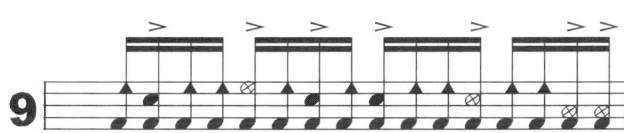

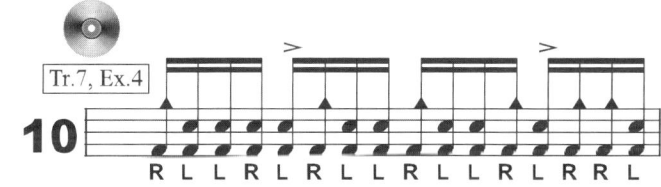

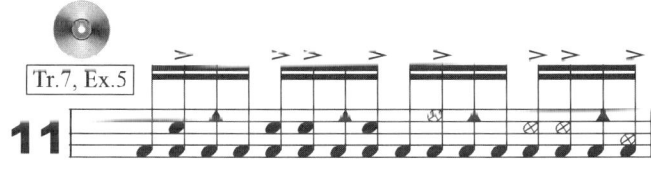

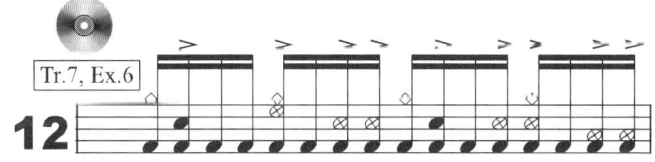

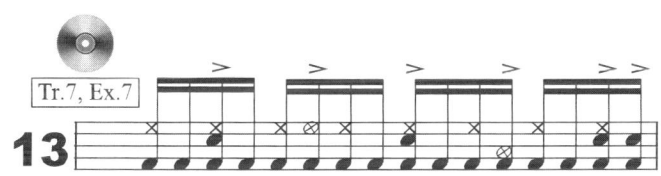

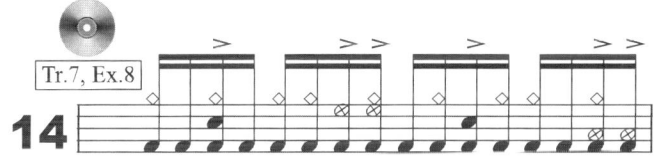

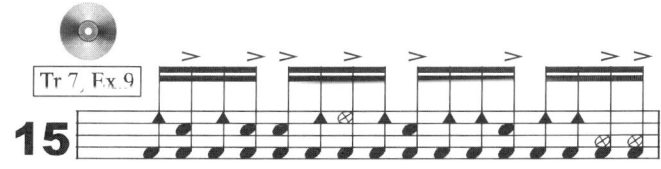

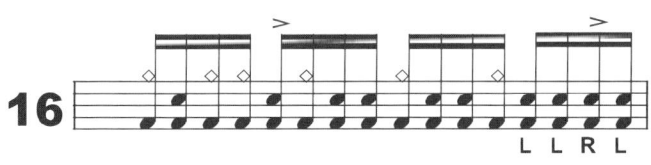

DOUBLE-PEDAL GOLD 21

HAND OVERLAYS

These hand patterns are to be played with continuous 16th-notes on the bass drum, singles, or doubles. I also recommend practicing these with as many bass patterns (including single pedal) as possible.

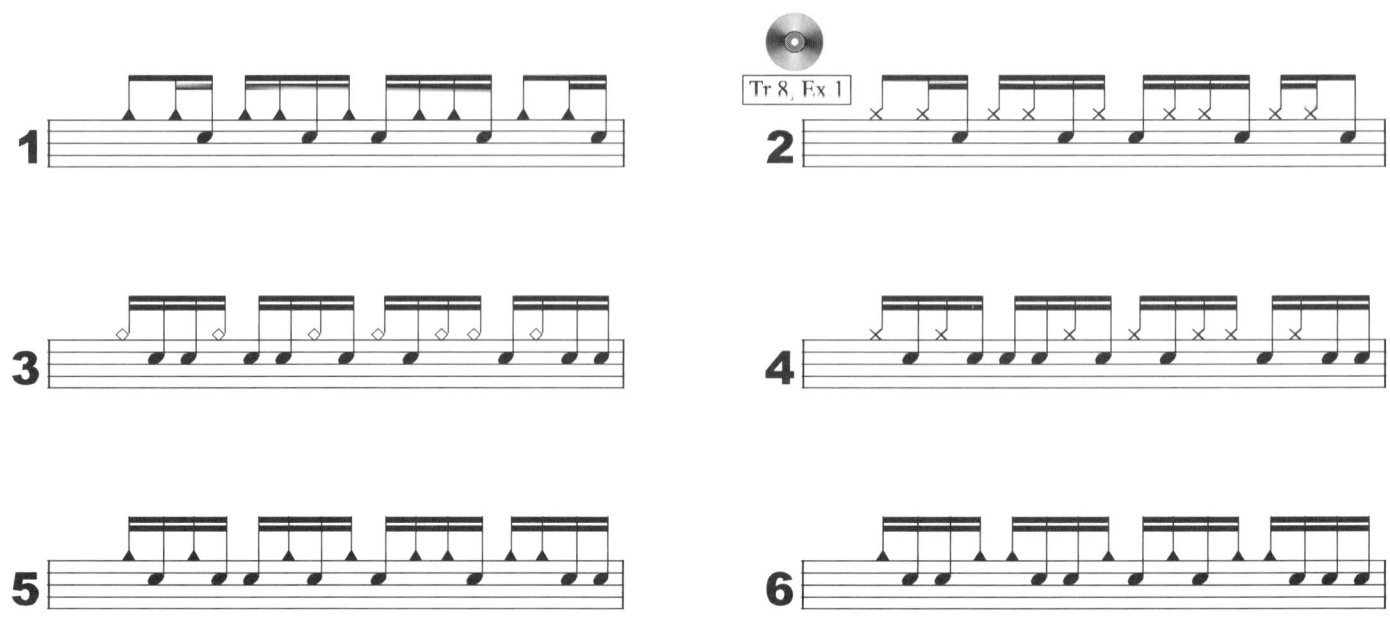

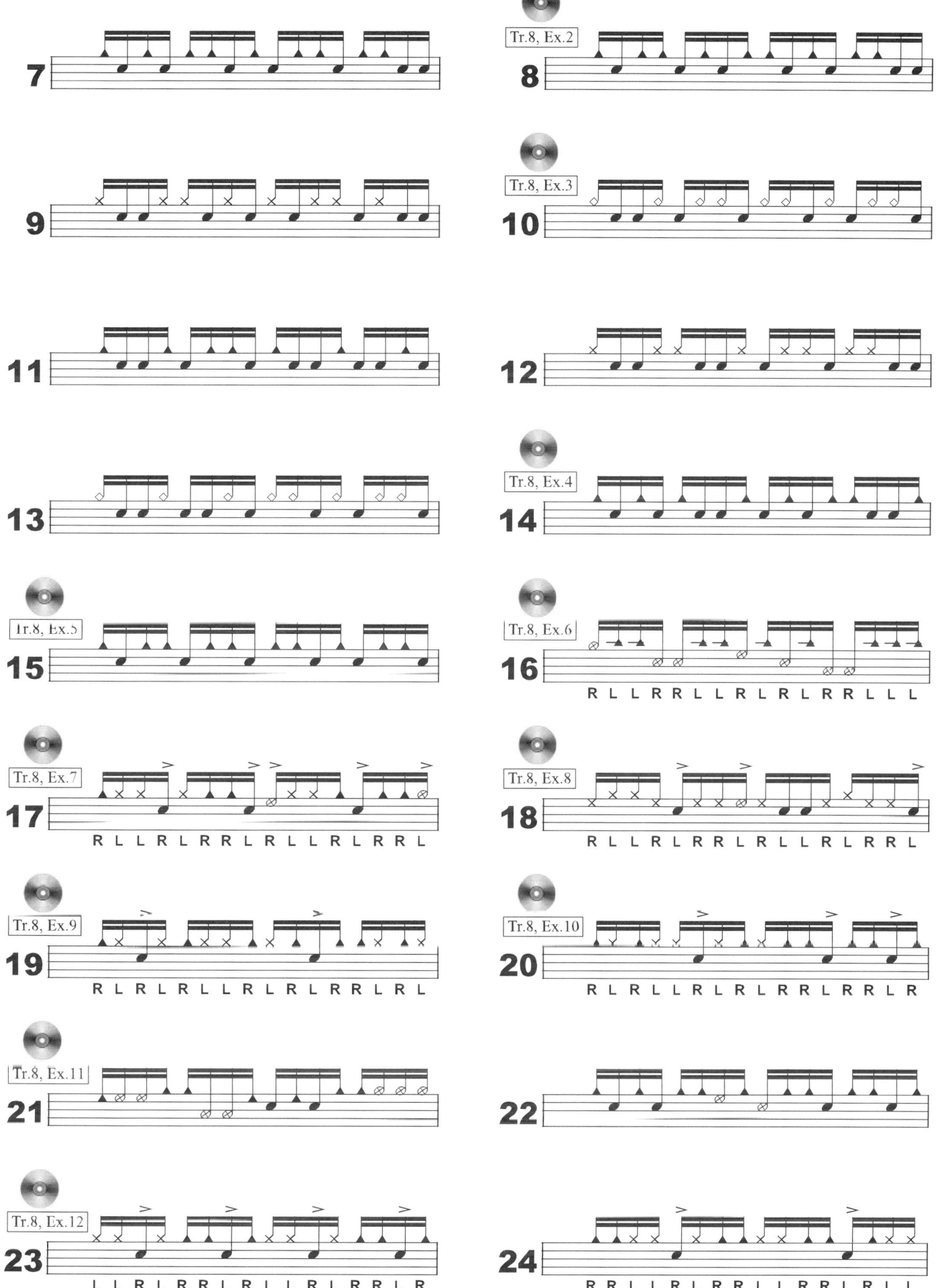

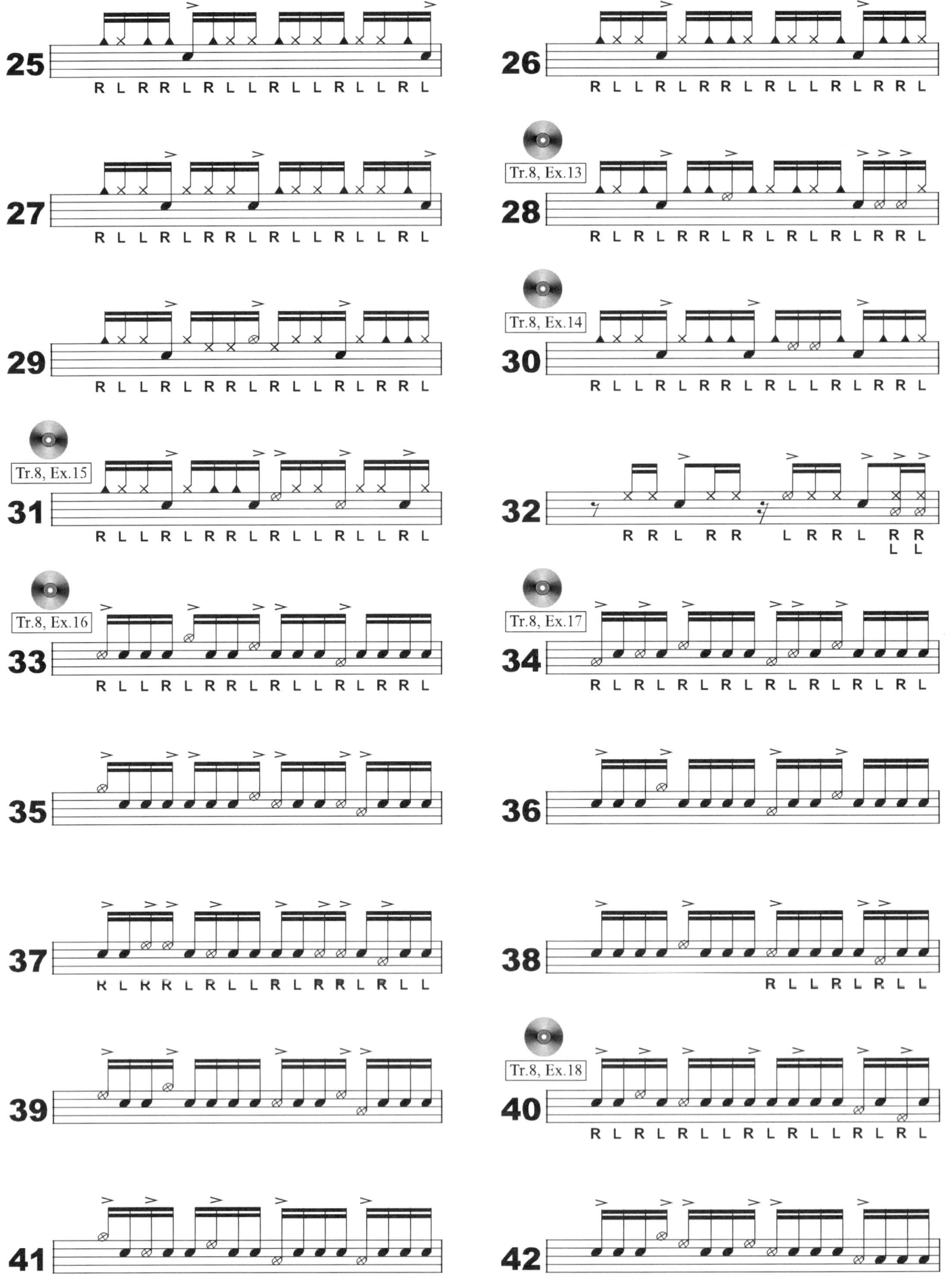

BEATS WITH 32ND-NOTES

Accents and stickings are for the hands only.

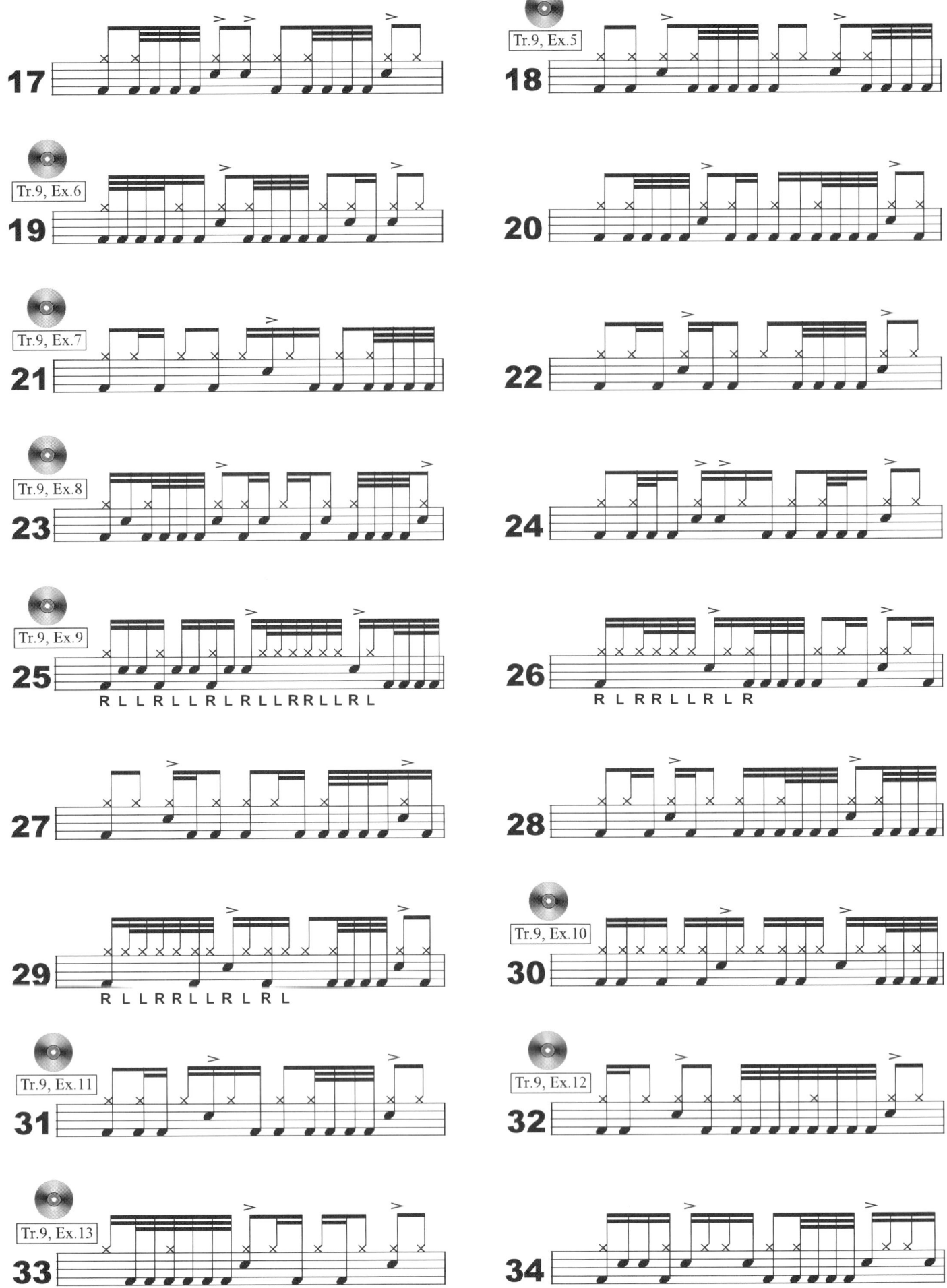

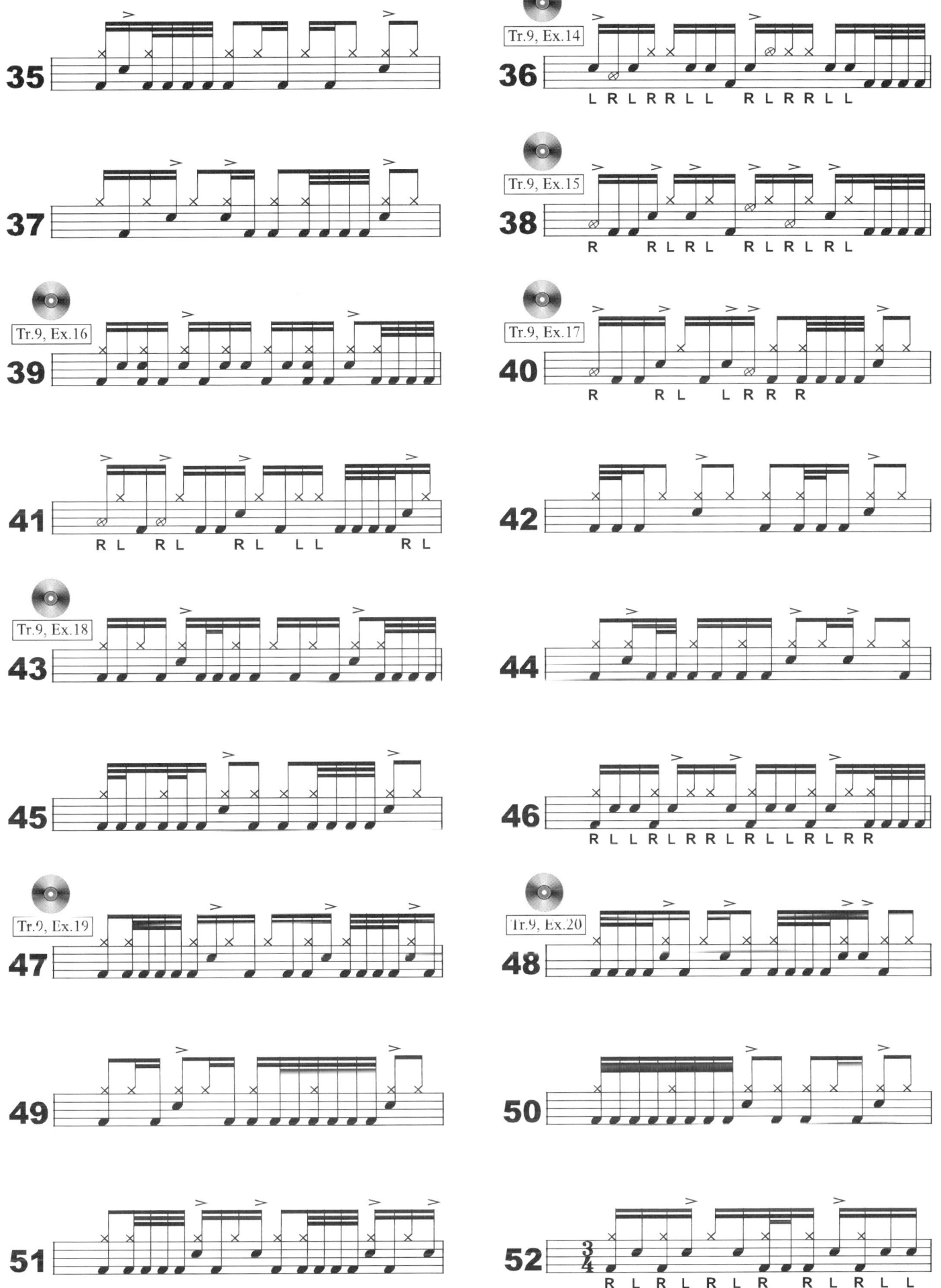

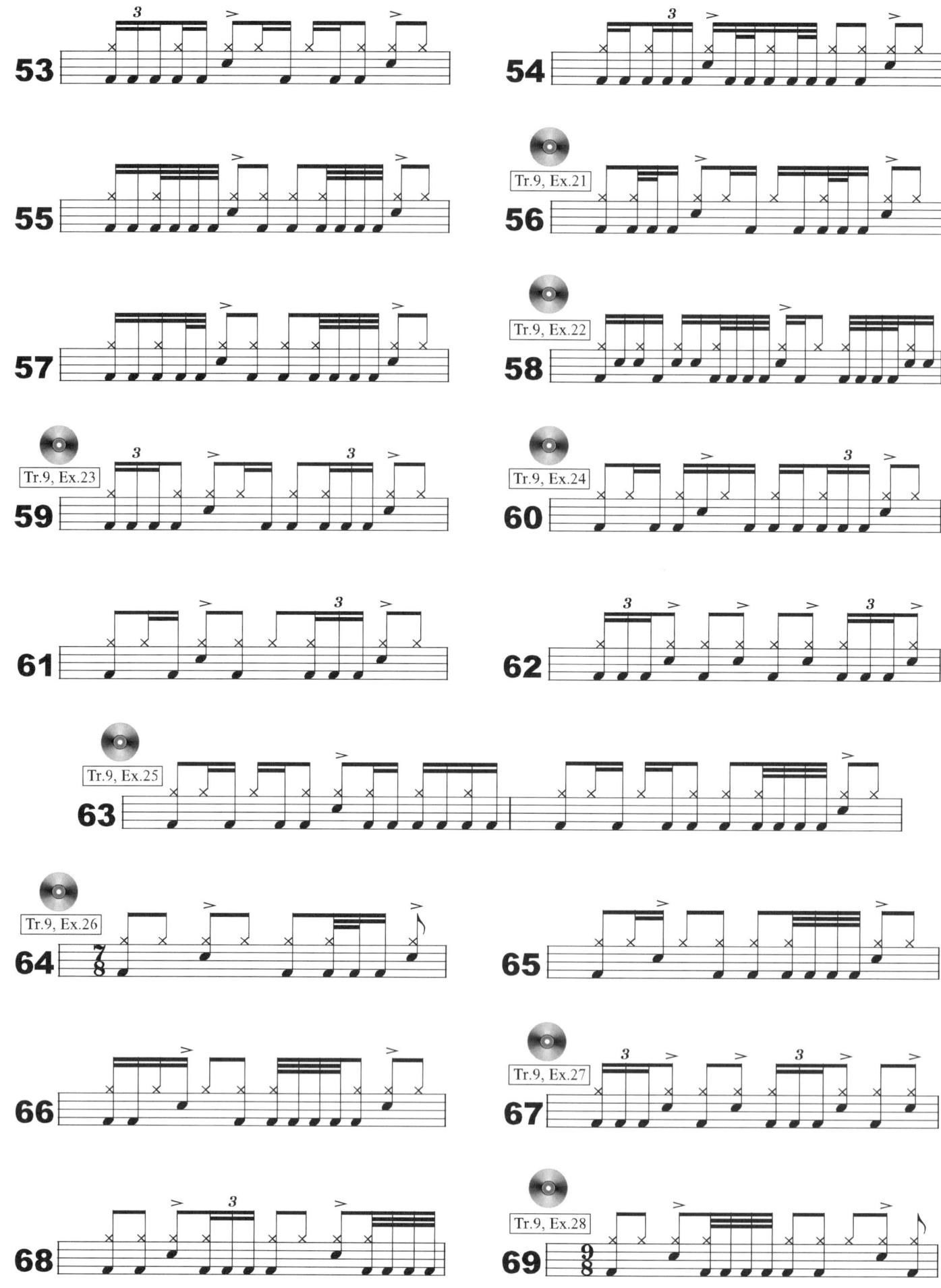

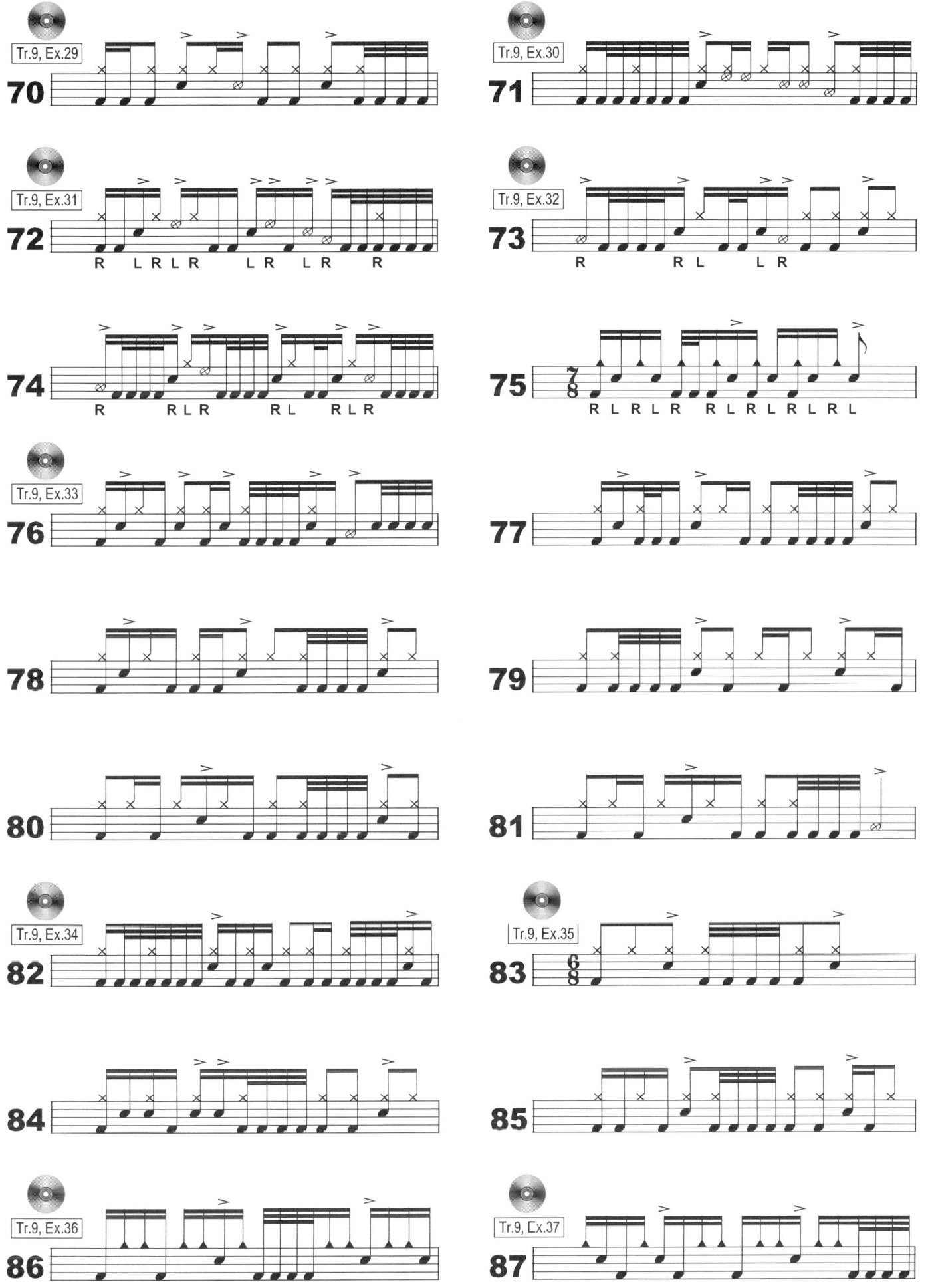

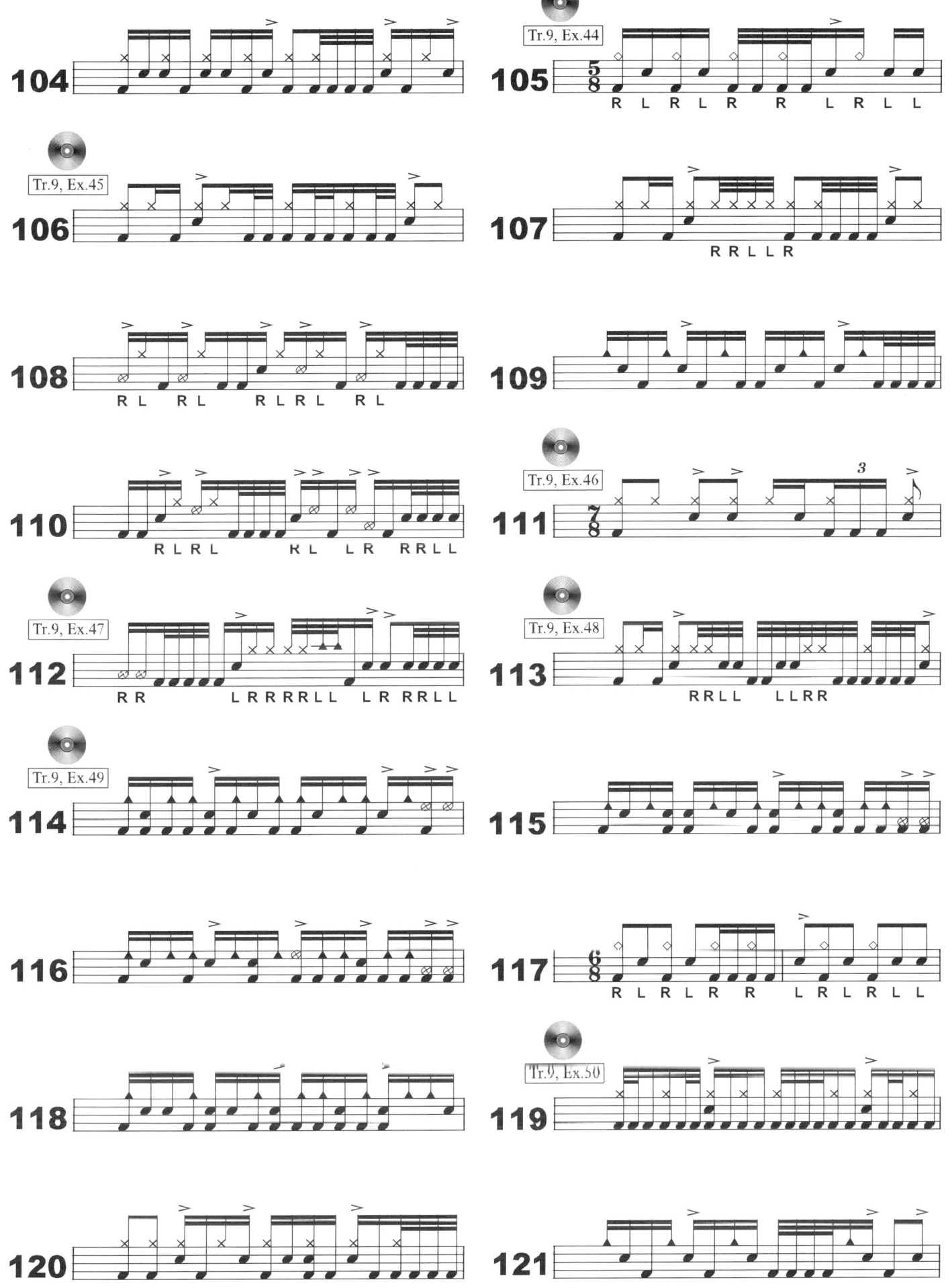

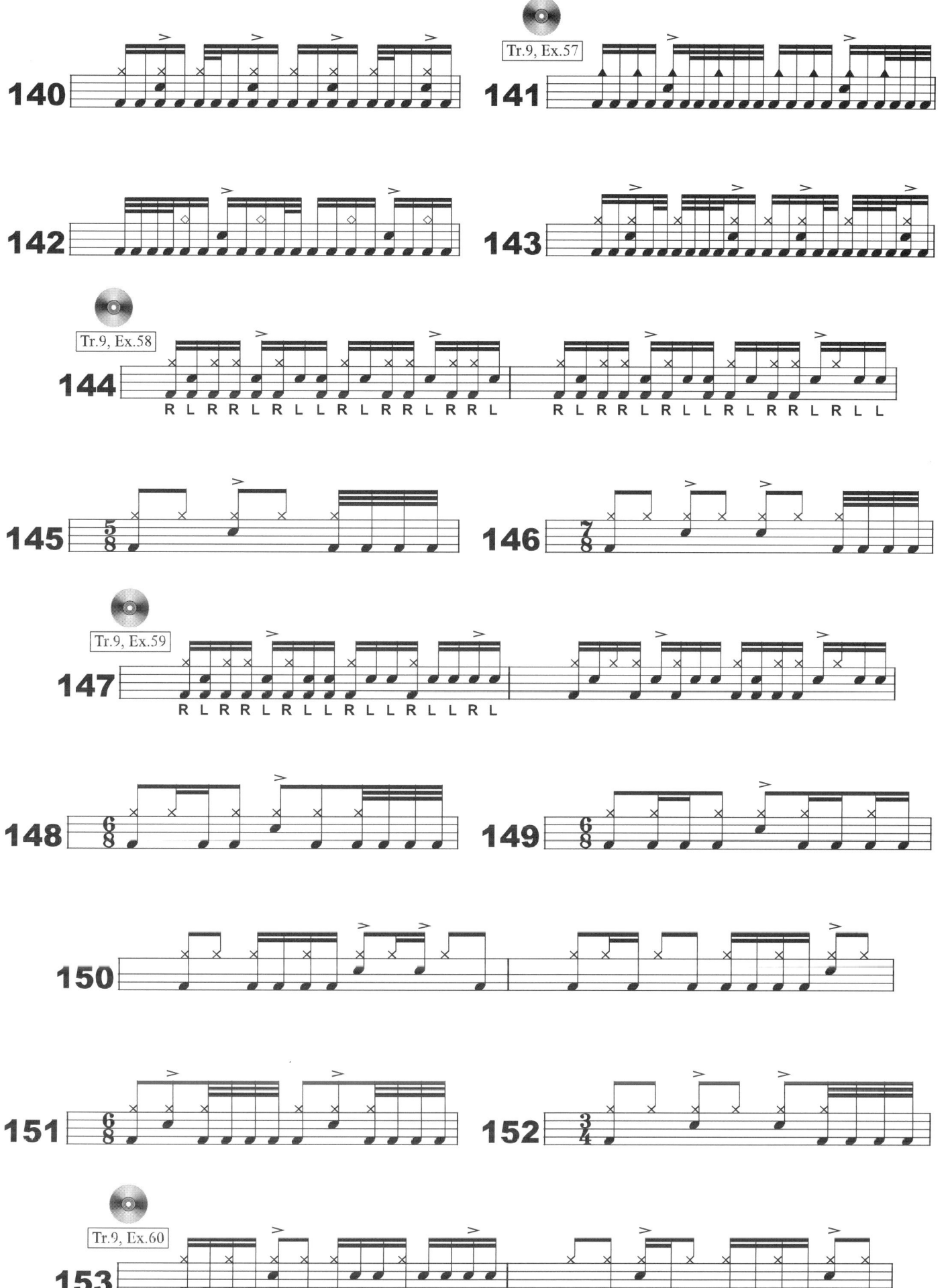

FOR MY SINGLE PEDAL FRIENDS

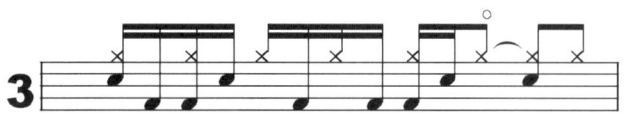

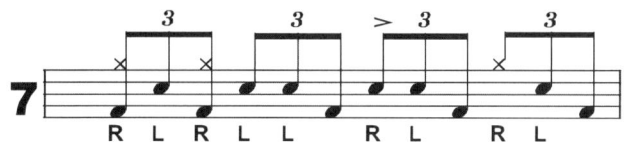
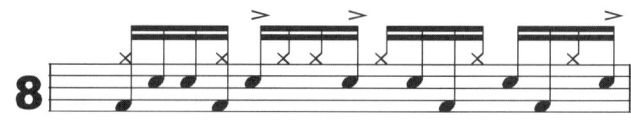

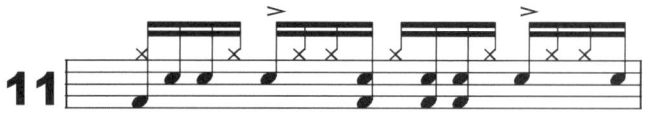
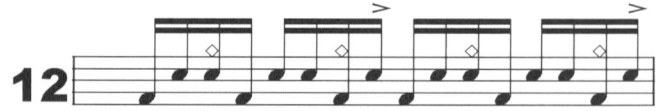

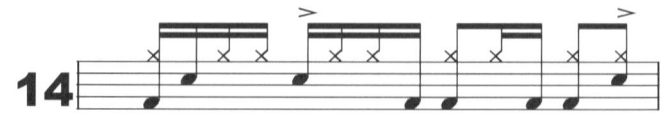

DOUBLE-PEDAL GOLD

THE PHILOSPHER'S STONE

On all solos, accents and stickings are for the hands only.

WHITE LIGHT

HIGH SPIN STATE

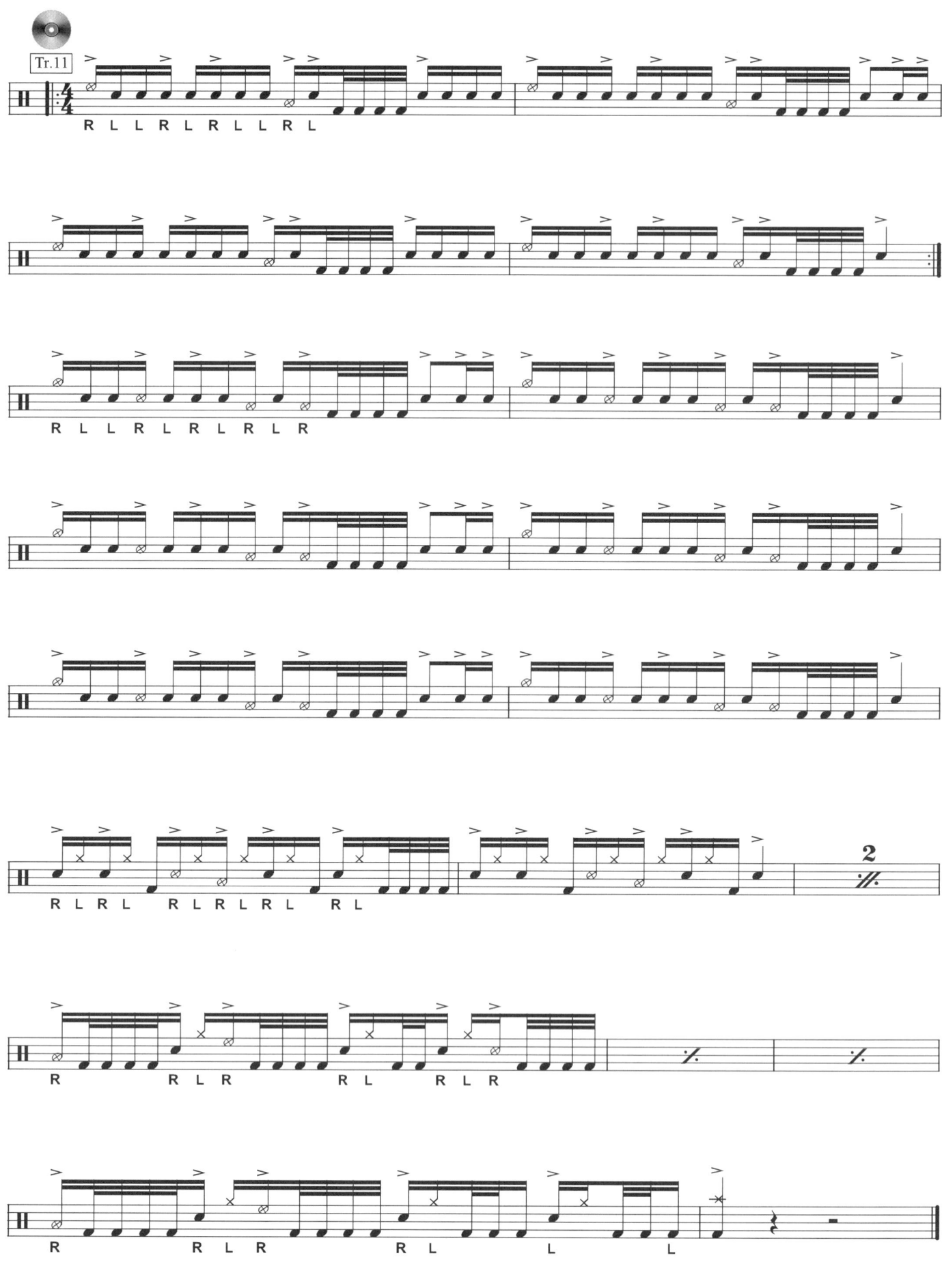

TO BROMOZO RIZ

ROCKOSIS

Also try playing R.H. and L.H. (cowbell and snare) as flam accents.

FOR COOKIE

FOR BLONDIE AND TOMMY

42 JOE MORTON

JASON

DR. WACKO

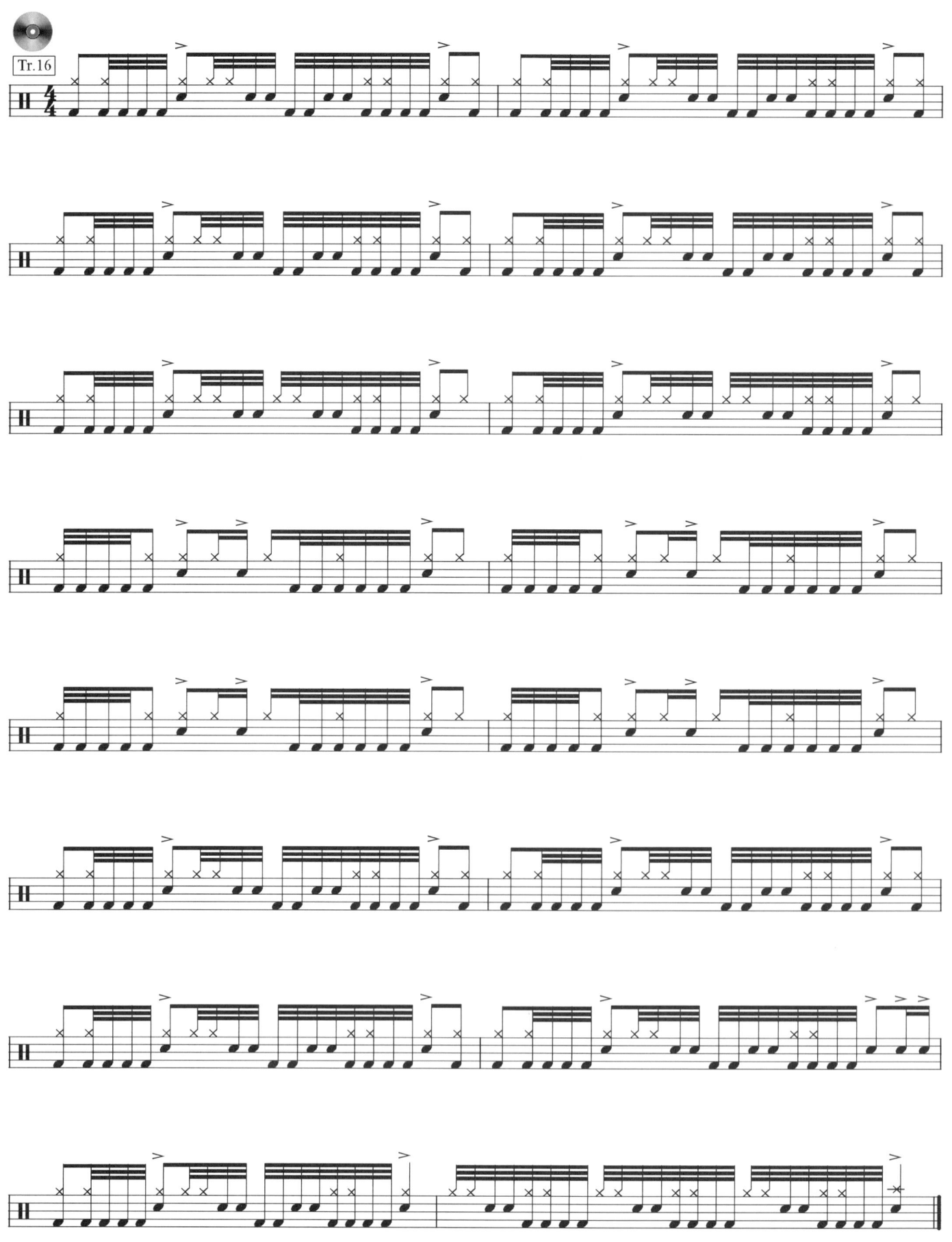

FOR MY NEXT LOVE

RIPSAW

METALITIS

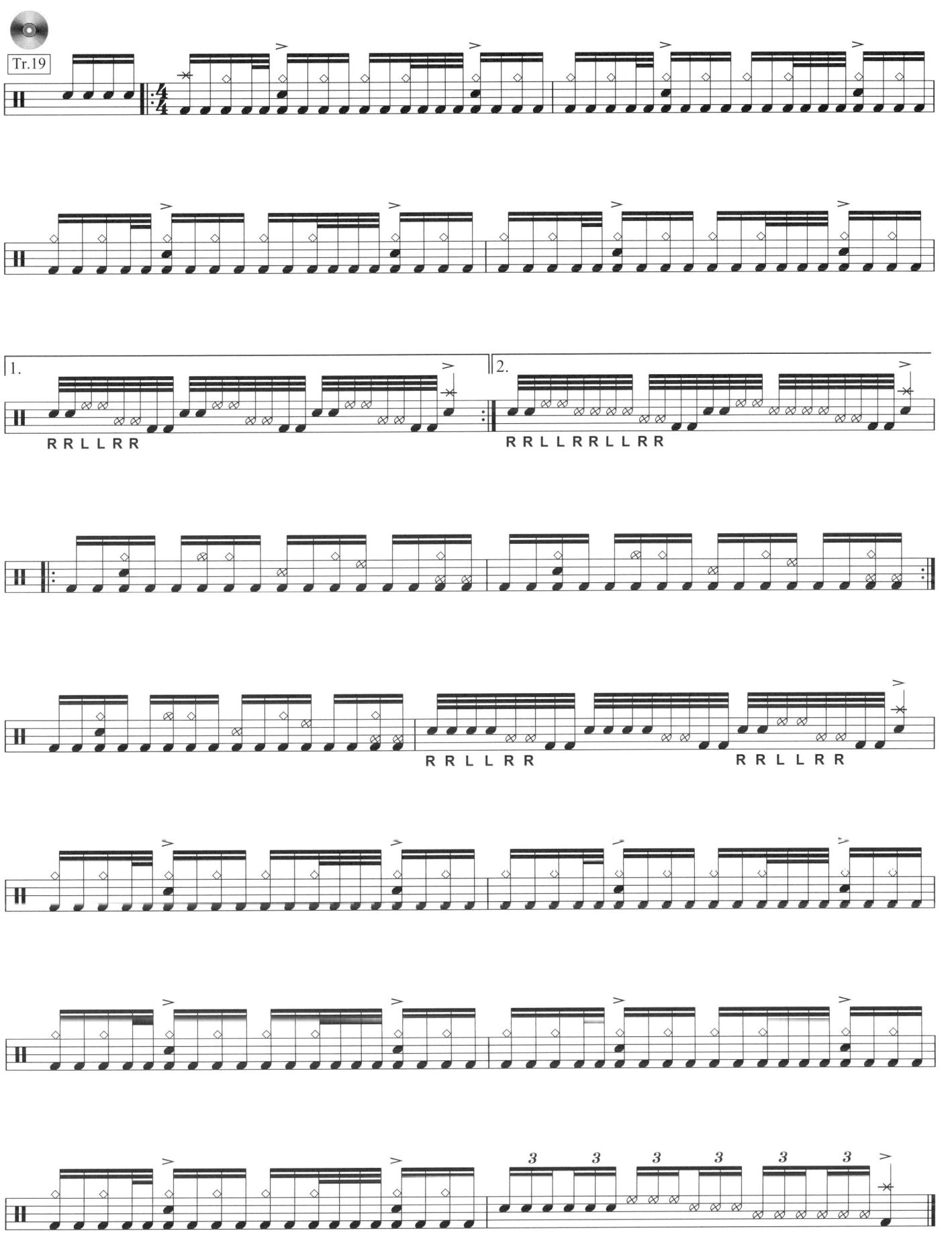

WHATUPWIDAT

48 JOE MORTON

I AM

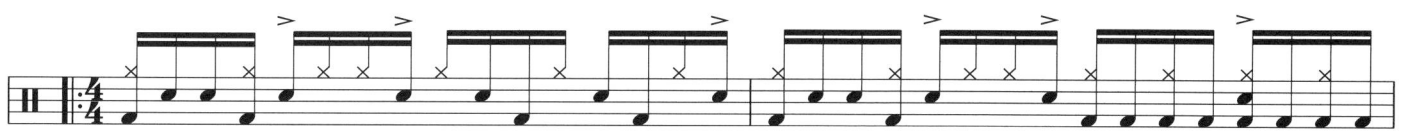
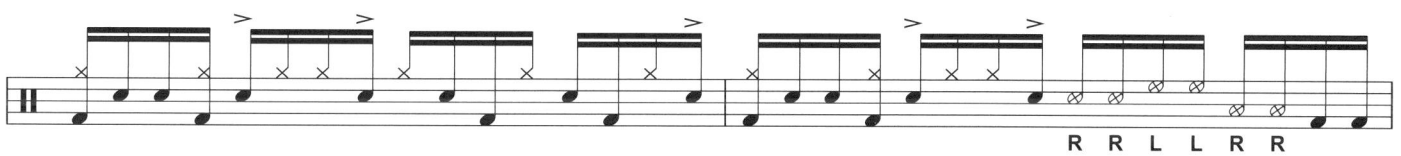

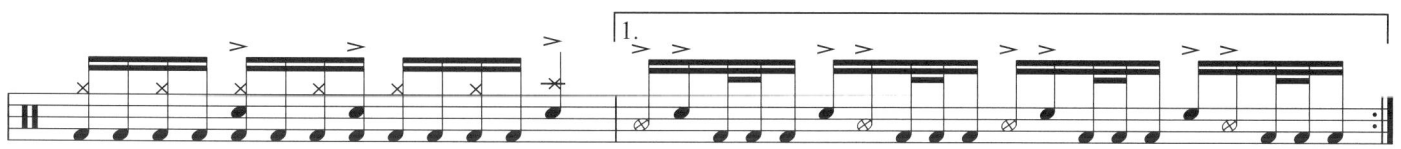
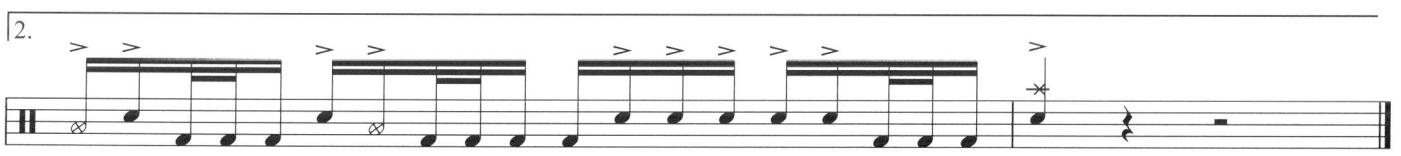

THE GRAIL

DECEMBER 21, 2012

FOR BOBBI

52 JOE MORTON

DOUBLE-PEDAL GOLD

SERENDIPITY

FIRE-STONE

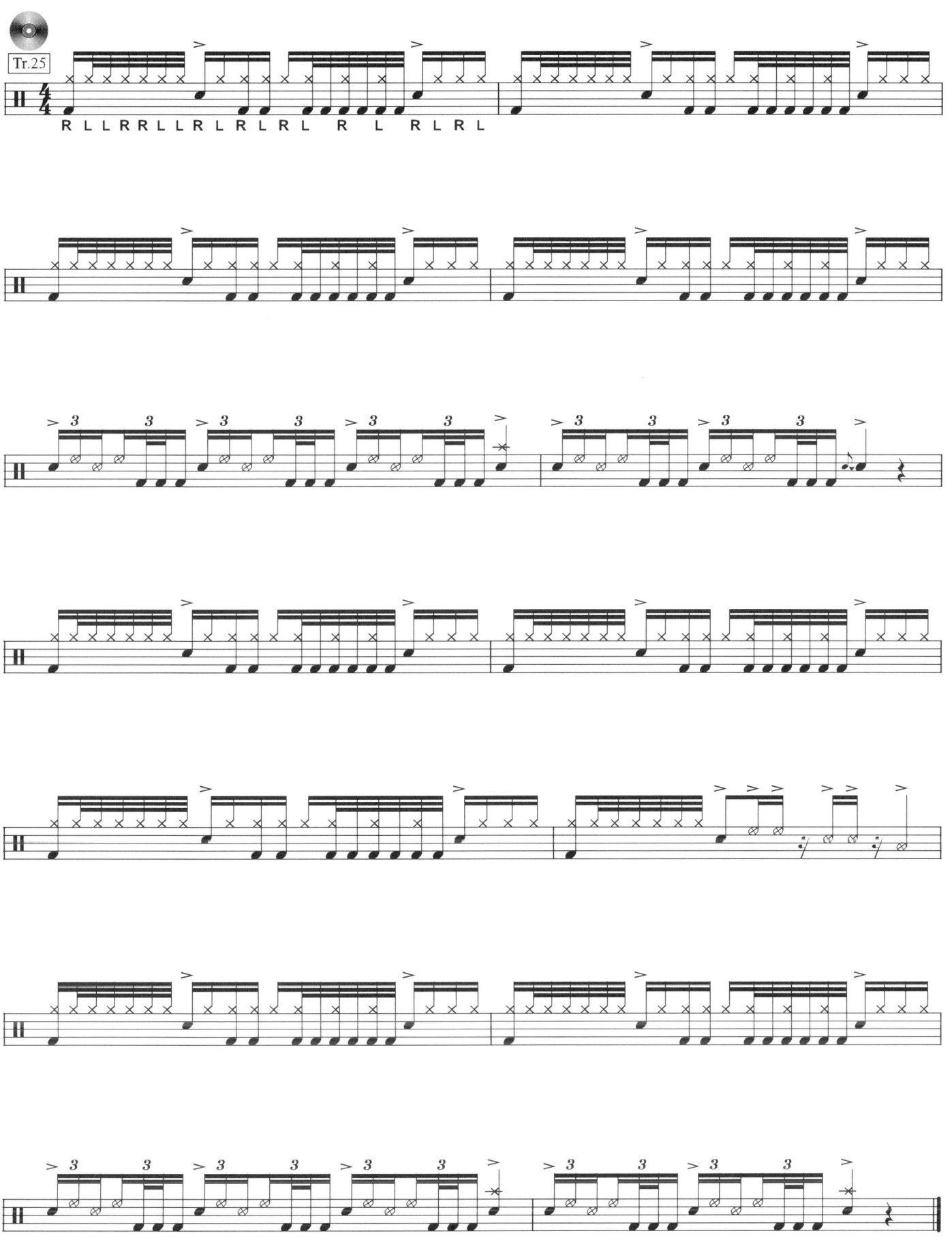

DOUBLE-PEDAL GOLD

FIELD OF THE BLESSED

56 JOE MORTON

MONATOMIC GOLD

THE D2D CONNECTION.
HUDSON MUSIC DVD'S · FROM DRUMMERS FOR DRUMMERS

CLASSIC ROCK DRUM SOLOS | THE ART OF PLAYING WITH BRUSHES | MODERN DRUMMER FESTIVAL 2006 | PHIL MATURANO AFRO-CUBAN DRUMMING... | MIKE PORTNOY IN CONSTANT MOTION | JOJO MAYER SECRET WEAPONS...

STEVE SMITH DRUMSET TECHNIQUE... | THOMAS LANG CREATIVE COORDINATION | JOHN BLACKWELL TECHNIQUE, GROOVING... | TOMMY IGOE GROOVE ESSENTIALS | NEIL PEART ANATOMY OF A DRUM SOLO | GREGG BISSONETTE MUSICAL DRUMMING...

HUDSON MUSIC DVDs

❑ THE ART OF PLAYING WITH BRUSHES (+CD & BOOKLET)	2 DISCS · 7 HRS : 15 MINS	❑ GENE KRUPA: SWING, SWING, SWING	1 DISC · 1 HR : 15 MINS
❑ CHRIS ADLER/JASON BITTNER: MD FESTIVAL 2005	1 DISC · 2 HRS : 35 MINS	❑ THOMAS LANG: CREATIVE CONTROL	2 DISCS · 5 HRS : 15 MINS
❑ CARTER BEAUFORD/VICTOR WOOTEN: MAKING MUSIC	1 DISC · 2 HRS : 55 MINS	❑ THOMAS LANG: CREATIVE COORDINATION	3 DISCS · 7HRS : 00 MINS
❑ GREGG BISSONNETTE: MUSICAL DRUMMING...	2 DISCS · 4 HRS : 20 MINS	❑ MODERN DRUMMER: FESTIVAL 2006 - SATURDAY	2 DISCS · 6 HRS : 20 MINS
❑ JOHN BLACKWELL: TECHNIQUE, GROOVING...	2 DISCS · 3 HRS : 15 MINS	❑ MODERN DRUMMER: FESTIVAL 2006 - SUNDAY	2 DISCS · 6 HRS : 30 MINS
❑ CLASSIC JAZZ DRUMMERS	1 DISC · 1 HR : 10 MINS	❑ MODERN DRUMMER: FESTIVAL 2006 - COMPLETE	4 DISCS · 12 HRS : 50 MINS
❑ CLASSIC JAZZ SOLOS VOLUME ONE	1 DISC · 1 HR : 00 MINS	❑ MODERN DRUMMER: FESTIVAL 2005	3 DISCS · 7 HRS : 10 MINS
❑ CLASSIC JAZZ SOLOS: VOLUME TWO	1 DISC · 1 HR : 15 MINS	❑ MODERN DRUMMER: FESTIVAL 2003	2 DISCS · 5 HRS : 50 MINS
❑ CLASSIC ROCK SOLOS	1 DISC · 2 HRS : 00 MINS	❑ MODERN DRUMMER: FESTIVAL 2000	1 DISC · 2 HRS : 50 MINS
❑ COLLINS, CHAMBERS, SMITH: SALUTE TO BUDDY RICH	1 DISC · 2 HRS : 25 MINS	❑ JEFF QUEEN: PLAYING WITH STICKS	1 DISC · 4 HRS : 00 MINS
❑ DRUMMER'S COLLECTIVE 25TH ANNIVERSARY	2 DISCS · 5 HRS : 25 MINS	❑ MIKE PORTNOY: IN CONSTANT MOTION	3 DISCS · 7HRS : 00 MINS
❑ PETER ERSKINE: AEMP LIVE IN NEW YORK	1 DISC · 1 HR : 45 MINS	❑ MIKE PORTNOY: LIQUID DRUM THEATER	2 DISCS · 3 HRS : 10 MINS
❑ PETER ERSKINE: LIVE AT JAZZ BALTICA	1 DISC · 1 HR : 15 MINS	❑ NEIL PEART: ANATOMY OF A DRUM SOLO	2 DISCS · 3 HRS : 20 MINS
❑ STEVE GADD: ADAA	2 DISCS · 6 HRS : 10 MINS	❑ BUDDY RICH: LIVE @ MONTREAL JAZZ FESTIVAL	1 DISC · 1 HR : 00 MINS
❑ LIONEL HAMPTON: JAZZ LEGEND	1 DISC · 1 HR : 10 MINS	❑ BUDDY RICH: AT THE TOP	1 DISC · 1 HR : 30 MINS
❑ HORACIO HERNANDEZ: MD FESTIVAL 2000	1 DISC · 1 HR : 05 MINS	❑ STEVE SMITH: DRUMSET TECHNIQUE/U.S. BEAT	2 DISCS · 4 HRS : 40 MINS
❑ TOMMY IGOE: GETTING STARTED ON DRUMS	1 DISC · 2 HRS : 20 MINS	❑ ULTIMATE DRUMMERS WEEKEND 10	1 DISC · 3 HRS : 55 MINS
❑ TOMMY IGOE: GROOVE ESSENTIALS	1 DISC · 3 HRS : 40 MINS	❑ ULTIMATE DRUMMERS WEEKEND 11	1 DISC · 3 HRS : 40 MINS

HUDSON LIMITED DVDs

❑ GAVIN HARRISON: RHYTHMIC HORIZONS	1 DISC · 2 HRS : 20 MINS	❑ JOJO MAYER: SECRET WEAPONS/MODERN DRUMMER	2 DISCS · 3 HRS : 00 MINS
❑ GAVIN HARRISON: RHYTHMIC VISIONS	1 DISC · 2 HRS : 20 MINS	❑ PAT PETRILLO: HANDS, GROOVE & FILLS (DVD+BOOK+CD)	1 DISC · 3 HRS : 00 MINS
❑ PHIL MATURANO: AFRO CUBAN DRUMMING...	1 DISC · 2 HRS : 11 MINS	❑ ULTIMATE DRUMMERS WEEKEND 2004	2 DISCS · 6 HRS : 00 MINS

HUDSON MUSIC MULTI-MEDIA PACKS

❑ TOMMY IGOE: GROOVE ESSENTIALS PLAY ALONG	BOOK+CD	❑ THOMAS LANG: CREATIVE COORDINATION	BOOK+CD
❑ JIMMY BRANLY: AFRO CUBAN DRUMMING	BOOK+CD	❑ TITO PUENTE: DRUMMING WITH THE MAMBO KING	BOOK+CD
❑ DAVID GARIBALDI: THE CODE OF FUNK	BOOK+CD+DVD-ROM	❑ TITO PUENTE: KING OF LATIN MUSIC	BOOK+DVD
❑ THOMAS LANG: CREATIVE CONTROL	BOOK+CD	❑ MAX WEINBERG: THE BIG BEAT	BOOK

SINCE THE DRUMMER-TO-DRUMMER CONNECTION IS THE STATE-OF-THE-ART IN DRUM EDUCATION, EVERY HUDSON MUSIC DVD, BOOK AND CD IS DESIGNED BY OUR AWARD-WINNING PRODUCTION TEAM TO FACILITATE D2D INTERACTION BETWEEN YOU AND THE WORLD'S LEADING DRUM ARTISTS.

AVAILABLE AT YOUR LOCAL DRUM SHOP OR MUSIC RETAILER.
DISTRIBUTED BY THE HAL LEONARD CORP. · (414) 774-3630
FOR FREE VIDEO CLIPS & MORE INFORMATION, LOG-ON TO WWW.HUDSONMUSIC.COM